Designing with
CorelDRAW
Be an expert!

The *Be an expert!* series consists of books which enable you to teach yourself in an easy and straightforward way how to work with a computer program.

You simply follow the theory and the practical exercises and ... No trouble! It works!
This series aims at being both pleasant and educational.

Also published in this series:
- Word Processing with Wordperfect
- Word Processing with Word for Windows
- Programming with QBasic

Koos Mebius

Designing with CorelDRAW

Be an expert!

Prisma *Be an expert!* first published in Great Britain 1994 by

Het Spectrum
P.O. Box 2996
London N5 2TA London

Translation: George Hall
Illustrations on page 10, 65, 100, 107, 131 & 156: Jurjen Tjallema
Production: LINE UP text productions

For the English translation
© 1994 Uitgeverij Het Spectrum B.V., Utrecht

No part of this book may be reproduced in any form, by print, photoprint, microfilm or any other means without written permission from the publisher.

ISBN 1-85365-356-X

British Library Cataloguing-in-Publication Data.
A catalogue record for this book is available from the British Library.

Contents

Before we begin   **9**
CorelDRAW   9
Why is CorelDRAW yelling?   10
The computer, MS-DOS and Windows   11
How to read this book   11
    CorelDRAW and the screen drawings   11
    Getting down to it   12
What is this book *not* about?   13
Enjoy yourself   13

1   The adventures of I.C. Talent   **14**
Starting CorelDRAW   14
What appears on the screen?   17
Where do I begin drawing?   19
Let's do it!   20
Eye movement   23
An eye as an eye   28
And smaller   28
I can't see anything!   29
A mouth is also quite handy   31
Don't forget your head   33
Printing the self-portrait   36
Saving the figure and exiting CorelDRAW   39

2   A visit to the plastic surgeon (and the solarium)   **42**
Making the lines thicker   44
Selecting several things at once   46
Trying out the Shape tool   48
And now a good strong skull in case of accidents   50
Making the entire head bigger   50
A stack of sheets   51

	Colouring in	52
	We can't fill this tooth	55
	Let's do the nose	55
	Smelling round the corner	60
	Saving the portrait under a new name	64
3	**An anti-dinosaur poster**	**65**
	Adjusting CorelDRAW a little	66
	The page settings	66
	The co-ordinates and the rulers	68
	Symbols	71
	Weren't dinosaurs quite large?	73
	Grab the magnifying glass	74
	Zooming in	75
	Zooming out	76
	A kick on the behind	77
	Mirror image	81
	Copying the dinosaur	84
	Into the rubbish bin	88
	Removing the lid using the Shape tool	90
	Making the rubbish bin opaque	94
	Fitting it all on the page	96
4	**Break**	**100**
	Help!	101
	Gridlines and guidelines	102
	Gridlines	102
	Guidelines	105
	Alignment	109
	The Shift key	110
	Skew	111
	Undoing rotation, skewing and mirroring	112
	Long live Bézier	112
	Curved lines using the Bézier pencil	113
	Drawing a straight line with the Bézier tool	117
	More about the Node Edit menu	120

	A straight line using the normal Pencil tool	122
	Converting a curve to a straight line	122
	More about the Shape tool	123
	Combining and grouping	126
	Importing	127
	On your marks ...!	130
5	**A small correction to the theory of evolution**	**131**
	Blending	133
6	**The microphone**	**137**
	Typing text and choosing the font	137
	Perspective	143
	The name of the school	144
	Artistic text and paragraph text	150
7	**Wallpapering**	**156**
	Two-colour patterns	157
	Full-colour patterns	162
	Creating a pattern yourself	163
	Rounding off	168
	Index	**169**

Before we begin

This book is about **CorelDRAW** which is a computer program you can use to make drawings. This kind of program is called a **graphic program**. Many graphic programs work in a very simple way: the screen resembles a sheet of paper and using the mouse pointer as a pencil or paintbrush, you can draw something on the 'paper'. This is very straightforward, but it's not possible to do much more than make elementary drawings.

CorelDRAW

CorelDRAW is different. When you work with CorelDRAW, you work in a way similar to the way an advertising artist works, or someone who makes posters. This kind of artist constructs his work out of separate pieces or components: lines, a freehand drawing, a photo, a frame, letters, coloured areas etc. He shifts sections back and forward, changes the size of the letters, reduces the size of the drawing, increases the thickness of the lines, and so on. Then he puts it all together.

This is the way you will work in CorelDRAW, but this takes place in a much easier way and you can do much more. You can use everything in your drawings such as lines, circles, your own drawings (created in CorelDRAW or in another program), drawings and symbols which are provided ready-made by CorelDRAW, all kinds of colours and shaded areas, and an abundance of letters. All these options can be moved, enlarged, reduced, mirrored, extended, copied etc. Almost everything you can imagine can be done!

Why is CorelDRAW yelling?

The CorelDRAW program is really called **Corel-DRAW!** (with an exclamation mark). But because this looks like shouting (if you know what we mean), we shall refer to **CorelDRAW** in this book, which is a little more peaceful.

The computer, MS-DOS and Windows

CorelDRAW is a program which runs under **Windows**. Therefore, to be able to work with CorelDRAW, it is advisable to know something not only about the computer and MS-DOS but also about Windows. In fact, you don't really have to **know** all that much, you only need to know how to **work** with the program.

Since this book is about CorelDRAW and not about MS-DOS and Windows, we shall presume that you know how to switch the computer on and you also know how to perform certain simple tasks in MS-DOS (such as copying and deleting files, and creating and moving to a directory). We also presume that you know how to start up Windows and you know something about how to operate it. When necessary, we shall give a short outline of how to carry out certain actions in MS-DOS and Windows, but we shall not explain everything.

How to read this book

CorelDRAW and the screen drawings

We presume that the CorelDRAW program has just been **installed** and nobody has used it as yet. If someone has been working with it already, certain **settings** may have been changed. This is no problem, but if you want to follow our examples closely, you should make sure that the **standard settings** are restored, in other words, the program is adjusted back to its original state. This is done as follows:

- From MS-DOS, go to the \CORELDRW\DRAW directory.
- Delete the CDCONFIG.SYS file (type: **del cdconfig.sys**). If you are not working on your own computer, you should ask permission first!

We have used a **VGA monochrome** screen when making the pictures and figures in this book. You can forget this immediately if you like but remember: **if you have a colour screen, some figures may appear different on your screen than they do in this book**. If the difference is very pronounced, we shall mention that in the text.

Getting down to it

In this book, we shall make a number of creations 'together'. In doing so, we shall explain how Corel-DRAW works, at the same time outlining the various possibilities provided. We can only really discuss the most important aspects of CorelDRAW because the program provides so many facilities that if we were to discuss all the small details, you would not see the wood for the trees.

In addition, we shall give many tips about how to do things more easily or more conveniently. These tips are shown in frames with a TIP symbol alongside, as displayed here:

What is this book *not* about?

Of course, that would be too much to mention. But in any case, it will **not** deal with several other programs which are also supplied along with the CorelDRAW package, such as CorelTRACE, CorelCHART and CorelSHOW. They will be discussed in separate books.

Enjoy yourself

CorelDRAW is a wonderful program. Have fun!

1 The adventures of I.C. Talent

We shall now get down to work with CorelDRAW, beginning with a captivating self-portrait.

Take a good look in the mirror.

Starting CorelDRAW

You must start CorelDRAW from Windows, which means that you have to start Windows before beginning with CorelDRAW.

Starting CorelDRAW 15

Windows is started as follows:

☞ Type **win** behind the DOS prompt (C:\>) and press **Enter**.

The Windows screen will appear after a moment. The words **Program Manager** should be shown at the top of this screen.

If everything has gone smoothly, a window similar to this one should be shown on the screen. Depending on which programs you have installed from your diskettes, additional companion programs may also be displayed here.

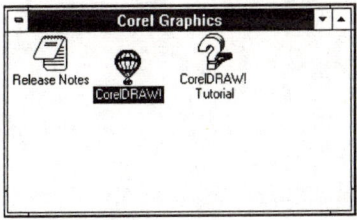

These small symbols are known as **icons**. We are dealing with CorelDRAW itself, therefore we require the CorelDRAW icon which looks like this:

I don't see the Corel Graphics window!

We are dealing with the **Corel Graphics** program group. If this is not shown, you can make it visible on the screen by clicking on the **Window** menu on the Program Manager menu bar. If you click on the word **Window**, the following menu appears:

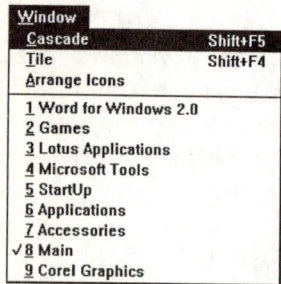

This menu may look a little different on your screen, depending on the programs which are installed on your computer.

Now click on the name **Corel Graphics**. The Corel Graphics window should then appear on the screen.

Starting up CorelDRAW is very simple:

☞ Double click on the CorelDRAW icon. *Double click* means that you should click on the left mouse button twice in rapid succession.

The screen displays a hot air balloon along with the letters CORELDRAW!. This is the **opening screen**. Then the **work screen** appears.

What appears on the screen? 17

 The CorelDRAW window is rather small

If the CorelDRAW window does not fill the entire screen, click on the small triangle pointing upwards in the top right-hand corner of the screen.

This enlarges the window as much as possible.

What appears on the screen?

The screen should look like this:

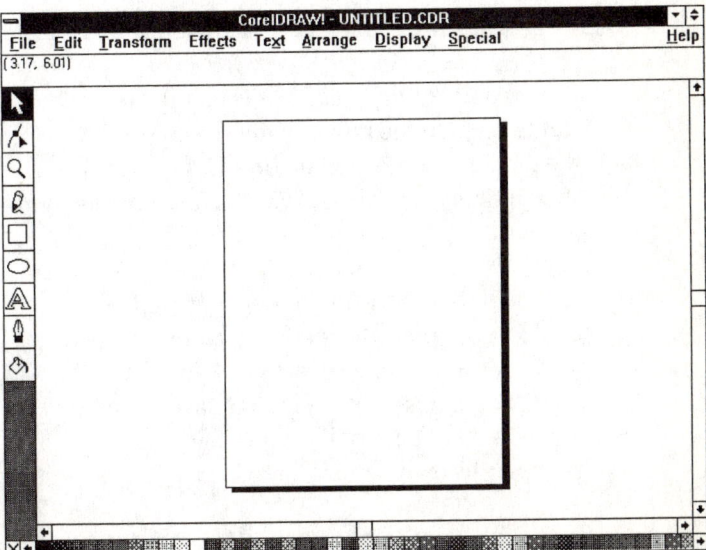

We shall now give a brief outline of the various components of the screen and their function. This makes it easier when referring to them later.

The **title bar** is shown at the top of the screen. This shows the name of the drawing on which you are working. In our example, there is no drawing as yet and therefore no name. The title bar shows UNTITLED.CDR. (The CDR is short for **CorelDRAW**, and is placed after the name of every drawing.)

```
CorelDRAW! - UNTITLED.CDR
```

The **menu bar** is shown under the title bar. This displays the menus provided by CorelDRAW. A menu is opened by clicking on the name of a menu in the menu bar. All Windows programs work in this way.

```
File  Edit  Transform  Effects  Text  Arrange  Display  Special                    Help
```

The area under the menu bar is referred to as the **status bar**. On the figure of the screen shown on the previous page, the numbers (**3.17, 6.01**) are shown on the status bar. We shall discuss this shortly.

At the left-hand side of the screen, a number of boxes are displayed containing various elements: an arrow, a pencil, a square etc. We refer to this collection of elements as the **toolbox**. Each box contains a certain 'tool' for making a drawing. Each has its own name:

Where do I begin drawing?

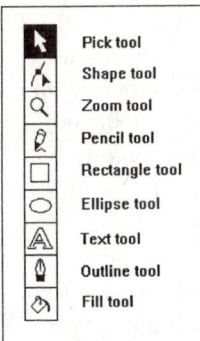

You will notice that the top box, the Pick tool, is darker (with a colour screen, this is dark grey). That means that this tool is **active**; in other words, this tool has been chosen and you can use it straightaway.

Along the bottom of the screen, there is a bar containing boxes in various shades of grey (or all sorts of colours if you have a colour screen). This is called the **colour palette**. You can already guess what you can do with this. We shall begin working with it in a few moments.

Just above the colour palette and also flanking the right-hand side of the screen, there are the so-called **scroll bars**. All Windows programs, and Windows itself, have these.

Where do I begin drawing?

The middle of the screen displays a rectangle with a 'shadow'. This rectangle represents a piece of paper on which you can draw. In this book, we shall refer to this rectangle as the **page**. The white area containing the page (thus everything between the status bar, the colour palette and the scroll bars) is called the **editing window**. You can draw anywhere in the editing window but only what is on the page will be printed.

You will also see the mouse pointer on the screen. We refer to this as the **cursor** in CorelDRAW. The cursor is now shown as a black arrow. Outside the editing window it takes on the shape of a **white** arrow:

Within the editing window, the cursor can assume many shapes. This depends on the tool you are using. The cursor is currently shown as a **black** arrow because the Pick tool is active:

Let's do it!

We can now begin with our self-portrait.

☞ Click on the **Ellipse tool** box.

This box now looks like this:

Let's do it! 21

This means that the Ellipse tool is **activated**. If you now move the cursor out of the toolbox, it changes from an arrow into a cross:

- ☞ Move the cross to the middle of the page.
- ☞ Press the left mouse button and hold it down.
- ☞ Move the cursor in various directions. You will see that you can create a circle which is larger, smaller, flatter or fatter.
- ☞ Release the mouse button when you have made a figure something like this:

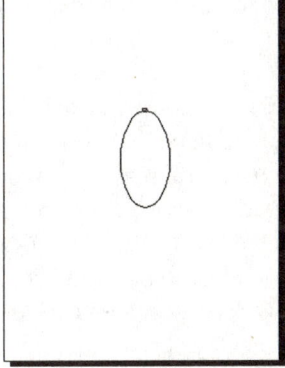

Mistake? Alt-Backspace!

*If you have released the mouse button at the wrong time or if you have made another mistake, that doesn't matter too much. Just press **Alt-Backspace**. This means press the **Alt** key, hold it down and press the **Backspace** key. Then release both keys. When you do this, your last action is cleared.*

*On some keyboards, this will only work if you press the **left** Alt key.*

Have you noticed that all kinds of information has been shown on the status bar in the meantime? We shall discuss this shortly.

The **Ellipse tool** is still active. This is indicated by the dark box and the form of the cursor which is still a cross.

While moving the mouse back and forward you have probably noticed that you can create both circles and ovals. You may not have realized it, but we have already drawn a **nose**. We shall now continue with the eyes. You are of course surprised how easy this all is, so the eyes should be **perfectly** round. This is done using the **Ctrl** key:

- ☞ Place the cursor above and to the left of the nose.
- ☞ Press the **Ctrl** key and hold it down.
- ☞ Press the left mouse button and hold it down.
- ☞ Move the cursor in various directions. You will see that you do not produce oval figures now,

only larger or smaller figures which are perfectly round.

☞ Release the left mouse button (and then the Ctrl key) when you have the circle you want:

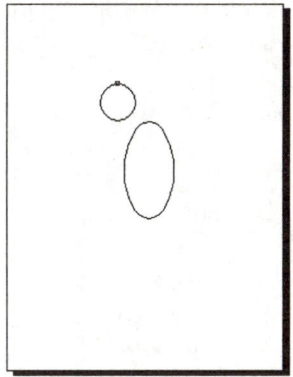

Draw the other eye in the same way. Make it a little larger and a little bit further from the nose.

Eye movement

Have you noticed that there is a small 'button' at the top of the circle? Perhaps you also noticed that this was also the case with the nose and the first eye? They have gone now. This button indicates that this figure is **selected** as we say.

What should we do to make this eye smaller and to place it a little nearer the nose? We could press Alt-Backspace and try drawing it again, but there is a more convenient way of doing this.

☞ Move the cursor to the toolbox and click on the **Pick tool** (the top box).

Two things happen:

1. The Pick tool box becomes dark and the arrow in the box becomes white. This indicates that this tool is active.
2. Black blocks appear all around the selected eye.

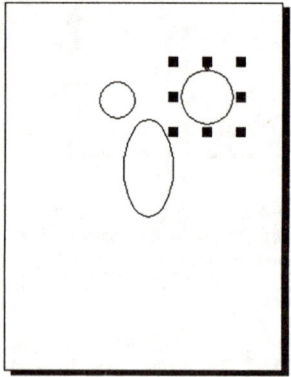

When you move the cursor out of the toolbox, it changes from a white arrow into a black arrow. This is also an indication that the Pick tool is active.

☞ Move the Pick tool to the circle with the blocks.
☞ Place the point of the arrow **at the edge** of the circle. Press the left mouse button and hold it down.

Eye movement

The blocks have disappeared. But as soon as you move the cursor, you will see this:

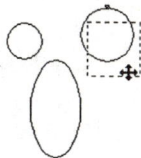

The dotted square indicates the section of the drawing which you are moving. In this case that is the selected eye. The eye is still shown at its old position on the screen, but it is actually in the process of being moved. It is stored invisibly in the square. The changed form of the cursor indicates that you are in the moving process.

- ☞ Move the cursor downwards until you come to under the nose.
- ☞ Release the left mouse button. The eye disappears from its old position and reappears at the position where you released the mouse button.

Have you clicked wrongly or clicked too many times?

*If you click **inside** or **outside** the circle instead of **on** it, the blocks also disappear, but the dotted square is **not shown** and the cursor is not in the form of a four-headed arrow. The eye is no longer selected. You can select the circle again by clicking **exactly on** the circle.*

If you see this:

*you must click exactly **on** the circle. You should then see the small black blocks again.*

 ### *Do you want to remove something from the screen?*

*If you have done something wrong, you can remove it by pressing Alt-Backspace. You already know that trick. But this is only possible if you have not drawn anything else in the meantime. What can you do if you want to delete something which is now 'out of reach' because you have drawn something else? In that case, you have to select it, which means clicking on the outside of the figure so that black blocks appear. Then you only need to press the **Delete** key to remove it. If you then regret this, you can recover it by pressing Alt-Backspace. So, no panic! You can arrange and rearrange without fear of losing too much.*

Eye movement

The screen page should now look something like this:

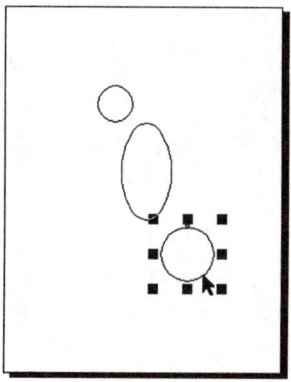

The eye is still selected. The black blocks indicate this.

- ☞ Click **away** from the circle outline. The block disappears: the selection is undone.
- ☞ Place the cursor a distance from the circle.
- ☞ Press the left mouse button and hold it down.
- ☞ Move the cursor downwards to the right. You will see that a dotted rectangle appears, becoming increasingly large:

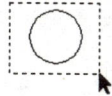

- ☞ Release the mouse button when the rectangle completely encloses the circle.

The circle is now selected again. This is thus another way of selecting a figure.

An eye as an eye

We shall put the eye in its proper place. Therefore, we have to 'pick it up' and shift it upwards.

- ☞ Place the Pick tool on the circle outline, press the left mouse button and hold it down.
- ☞ Move the eye to the proper place and release the mouse button.

And smaller

We haven't finished yet; the eye is much too large. But that is easily altered.

The eye is still selected. Place the cursor on the small block in the upper right-hand corner. The cursor changes into a cross.

- ☞ Press the left mouse button and hold it down. The blocks disappear just as with moving.
- ☞ Move the cursor upwards to the right. The cursor changes into diagonal four-headed arrows. A dotted square also appears which becomes larger as you move the cursor.

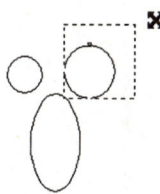

☞ Adjust the dotted square until it is roughly the same size as the first eye. Then release the mouse button.

In this way you can enlarge or reduce the size of any selected figure.

I can't see anything!

We shall now draw the eye pupils.

☞ Click on the **Ellipse tool** in the toolbox.
☞ Position the cursor somewhere in the right eye (left for the viewers!).
☞ Draw a small circle using the **Ctrl** key.

Everything's going fine. We have just drawn a small circle which is still automatically selected (because it's just been drawn). The small bobble at the top indicates this. But how can we make the pupil black? This is done by means of the colour palette.

☞ Click on the box at the extreme left of the colour palette (black). This is the result:

We could do the same for the other eye, but we shall now apply a different method just to show the possibilities. We shall **duplicate** the pupil. This is done by means of the **Ctrl-D** key combination.

☞ Press **Ctrl-D** (press **Ctrl**, hold it down and then press **D**; then release both keys).

A **copy** of the first pupil is created. You now only have to move it to the proper position.

☞ Activate the **Pick tool**. You will see that the second pupil is selected (although you could already see that by the bobble at the top of it).
☞ Click on the pupil and hold the left mouse button down. You do not need to click on the outline this time because the figure is filled in.
☞ Place the pupil in the second eye.
☞ Click somewhere outside one of the figures you have drawn.

A mouth is also quite handy 31

Your self-portrait will now look something like this:

A mouth is also quite handy

Of course, a face without a mouth doesn't say much. We shall draw this using the **Pencil**.

☞ Click on the **Pencil** in the toolbox:

The box becomes dark and the cursor changes to a cross.

☞ Move the cursor to where the mouth should begin, press the left mouse button and hold it down. Draw the mouth as follows:

☞ Release the left mouse button.

As soon as you have released the mouse button, you will notice that a few small buttons appear on the line:

These buttons are similar to the button which appears at the top of a circle when you draw it. We refer to these buttons as **nodes**. The line which you have just drawn is called a **curve**. In this case, it really is a curve, but even if that were not the case, it would still be called a 'curve' in CorelDRAW. This may seem a bit confusing but accept it for the time being. We shall explain this all in chapter 4.

A curve always has at least two nodes, one at the beginning and one at the end. Mostly there are also nodes in between, depending on the way the line goes.

☞ Now draw a tooth in the same way:

You will see a number of nodes here too as soon as you release the mouse button.

☞ Now click on the **Pick tool**. Click away from the tooth to ensure that the tooth is no longer selected.

Don't forget your head

Our self-portrait is not exactly Rembrandt, but we could claim that it is modern art. In that case, it's quite acceptable to have a square head.

☞ Click on the **Rectangle tool**:

The cursor becomes a cross again. You can now draw a square or a rectangle.

☞ Click above and to the left of the drawing and 'drag' a rectangle around it. When you release the mouse button, the portrait should look something like this:

The adventures of I.C. Talent

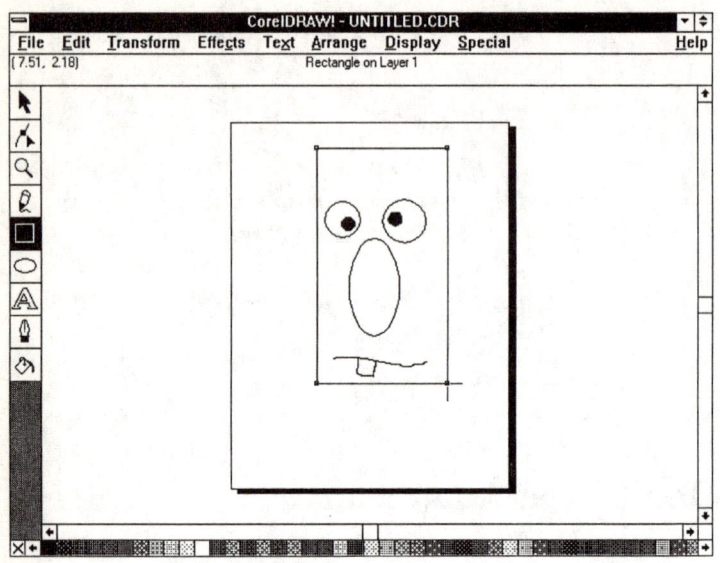

☞ Click on the **Pick tool**.

If the rectangle is not quite at the right place, you can move it. You already know how to do that. If you want to make it larger or smaller, you know how to do that too. But what do you do if you want to make the rectangle **longer, shorter, narrower or wider**, in other words, you want to squeeze or stretch it? This is done in the same way as with enlarging or reducing, except you should place the cursor on the **in between** blocks instead of on the blocks at the corners.

☞ Move the cursor to the **middle** block of the bottom three blocks. The cursor changes into a cross.
☞ Press the left mouse button and hold it down.

Don't forget your head

☞ Move the cursor downwards. You will see that the head is stretched: it becomes longer but not broader (despite the fact that you can move the cursor to the left and right).

☞ Move the cursor upwards and place the bottom line of the rectangle roughly where it was.

You can also try this out with a black block at the left- or right-hand side of the head.

Click away from the figure when you are finished so that nothing is selected. This can also be done by pressing **Esc**.

The Ctrl key: very useful

*If you want to make a real square (thus with sides of equal length), you should hold down the **Ctrl** key when drawing the square. You performed a similar action with the Ctrl key when making a perfect circle.*

The Ctrl key also enables you to carry out another interesting action. If you hold the Ctrl key down when enlarging or reducing a figure, the enlarging or reducing process takes place in large steps. This is done in jumps which make the figure exactly two, three, four etc times as large or as small. This also works in the same way for stretching or squeezing.

Printing the self-portrait

It is now time to bring our drawing on to the market. We shall print it:

☞ Press **Ctrl-P**.

The window which appears on the screen depends on the printer installed. It will look something like this:

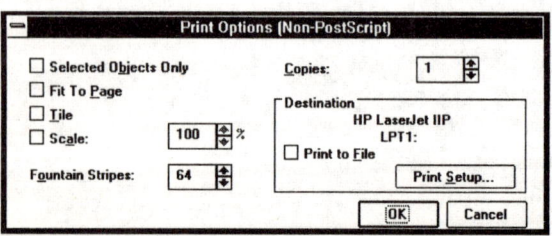

Printing the self-portrait

☞ Click on **OK**.

Now CorelDRAW begins printing. Another window indicates the progress of the printing:

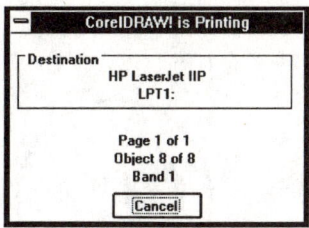

It may take some time before the drawing is complete, but as you see it is a masterpiece.

Saving the figure and exiting CorelDRAW

You probably know about the meaning of saving. You save the drawing in a **file** on the harddisk so that it is not lost when you switch off the computer.

☞ Click on the word **File** on the menu bar. The File menu opens:

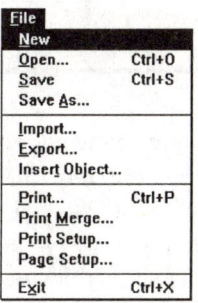

In this menu, you can select either **Save** or **Save As**. If you have already given a drawing a name, you can save the drawing again under the same name by selecting **Save** (or by pressing the key combination **Ctrl-S**). If you want to save the drawing under a **new** name, select **Save As**. In this case, because we have not yet given a name to the drawing, it does not matter which option we choose.

☞ Select **Save As**.

The following dialog box appears:

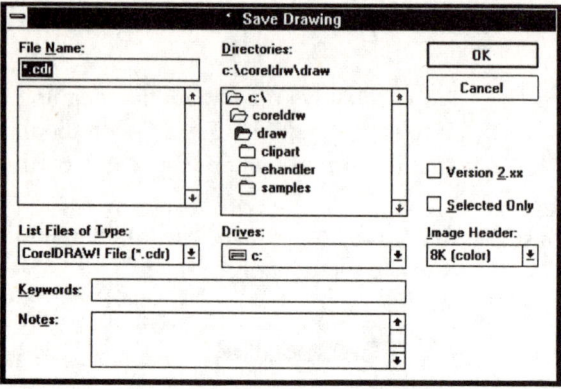

In the middle section of the window, under **Directories**, you can select a different directory if you like. This is done by double clicking on the directory you want when it is shown in the Directories box. If you want to save the drawing on a diskette for instance instead of on the harddisk, click on the arrow pointing downwards in the **Drives** box and then click on A: or B:. If you are familiar with Windows, you will know how this is done. If it is difficult at this stage, it will do no harm to ask a friend, parent or teacher who knows more about Windows.

Let's assume that no problems arise.

☞ Type: **selfport**.

This is the file name. You probably know that file names must not have more than eight letters or numbers (or a combination of these). CorelDRAW always automatically places **CDR** behind the file name.

☞ Press **Enter**.

The **Save Drawing** window disappears again.

We can now close down CorelDRAW. Nothing will be lost. Even if you want to continue, it is always convenient to know how to open and close down your programs.

CorelDRAW is a Windows program and therefore it is closed down just as other Windows programs by pressing the **Alt-F4** key combination. You can also select the **Exit** option from the **File** menu if you prefer. Or you can press the key combination **Ctrl-X**.

☞ We select **Alt-F4**.

CorelDRAW is closed down and you move to the Windows screen.

2 A visit to the plastic surgeon (and the solarium)

In this chapter we shall **open** the self-portrait (in other words, show it on the screen) and give it a good going over.

☞ Start CorelDRAW again.
☞ Open the **File** menu by clicking on the name on the menu bar.

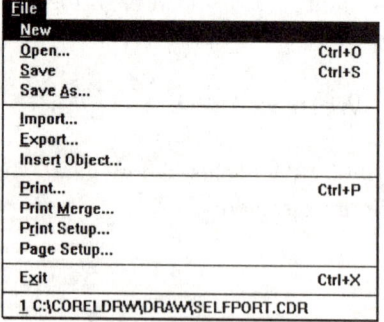

As you see, the name SELFPORT is shown at the bottom of the menu options. If you click on this name, the file is opened straightaway. The names of the last four files which you have loaded are always shown here. In our case, we have only created and used one file, so only one name is displayed. We shall not open this file by clicking on the name; we shall use a different method which provides more possibilities.

☞ Click on **Open**. The following window appears:

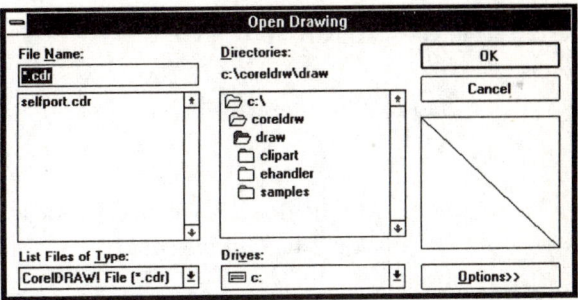

If you click once on the name of the **selfport.cdr** file, the box with the diagonal line at the right side of the window will display a rough image of the drawing:

This is very useful if you have a lot of drawings.

☞ Double click on the name of the drawing (**selfport.cdr**) to load the drawing.

The self-portrait is now displayed on the screen. The title bar shows the name of the opened file:

CorelDRAW! - SELFPORT.CDR

Making the lines thicker

We shall begin by making the lines of the self-portrait thicker.

☞ Select the nose. Black boxes appear.
☞ Click on the **Outline tool**.

Several boxes suddenly appear. We call this a **pop-up menu**. The boxes have the following significance:

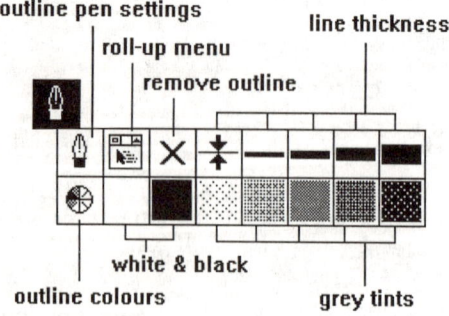

We shall encounter these boxes shortly.

The drawing has been made using the standard line thickness which is the thickness of the line between the arrow pointing downwards and the arrow pointing upwards. At the extreme right of the status bar you will see **Outline: 0.003 inches**.

Making the lines thicker 45

The nose looks rather puny in our drawing; we want to give it more emphasis.

☞ Click on the pen which looks just like the Outline tool except that it is shown inversely. The following dialog box appears:

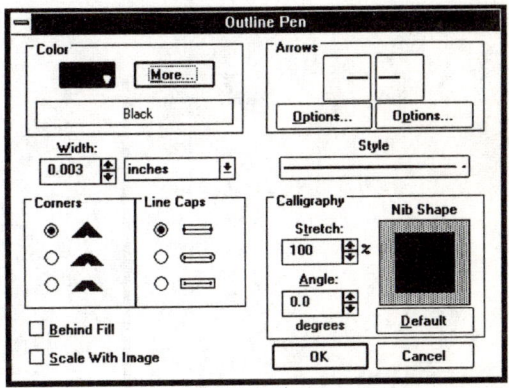

☞ Click on the arrow pointing upwards in the box under Width:

The value is increased. You can select any value you like. Select **0.203** for instance. (You can also type a value in this box by clicking on it and typing the required numbers.) Click on OK. The new thickness is immediately applied to the drawing.

The nose has become a real whopper! This is really too much. We shall have to adjust it a little.

- ☞ Select the nose again if it is not already selected.
- ☞ Click on the **Outline tool**.
- ☞ Click on the middle line thickness.

The nose is immediately readjusted. It remains a prime specimen but at least it's a bit more acceptable now.

Selecting several things at once

You are probably aware that the various components of the pictures are placed 'loosely' on the page. For instance, you can select the nose and move it or enlarge it without this process having any effect on the rest of the drawing. This makes CorelDRAW rather special. The **Paintbrush** program for example (the graphic program supplied along with Windows), is quite different. With Paintbrush you only draw **points** on the page, and

Selecting several things at once

points which form a circle for instance have no real relation to one another. They only lie on the page in such a way that they resemble a circle.

When we refer to **components**, we mean the various separate units which make up the drawing, such as an eye or the nose etc. In fact a component may be any part of the drawing: a circle, a line, a square, even a letter or a word (as we shall discuss later).

Up until now we have selected one thing at a time, but it is possible to select **several components at one time**. This can be done in two ways:

1. By dragging a frame around what you want to select after clicking on the **Pick tool**. This type of frame is called a **marquee rectangle**.
2. By pressing the **Shift** key, holding it down and clicking on the components you want to select, one by one. If you click on a component again (holding down the Shift key), it is removed from the selection.

We shall now select the whole face **without** the head outline:

☞ Drag a frame around the whole portrait.

You will see black blocks around the head only, but the nodes on all components indicate that they have all been selected.

☞ Press the **Shift** key and hold it down.
☞ Click on the outline of the head.

The status bar shows: **7 objects selected on Layer 1**. Forget about the 'Layer' for the time being; the '7 objects' indicates what you have selected.

We shall give all these lines the same thickness as the nose.

☞ Click on the **Outline tool** and select the line with the middle thickness.

Trying out the Shape tool

Isn't the head rather sharp? It's maybe all right for carrying trays but not much use for heading goals. Perhaps we can do something about it using the **Shape tool**.

Trying out the Shape tool 49

☞ Select the head.
☞ Click on the **Shape tool**.

As soon as you move the cursor out of the toolbox, it assumes the following shape:

The Shape tool enables you to change the shapes of things. You can change the size of components and also stretch and squeeze them using the Pick tool, but the Shape tool actually provides more possibilities. We shall now give an example of this.

☞ Position the cursor on one of the corners of the head (the bottom right-hand corner for instance) and place it on the small square node.
☞ Press the left mouse button and hold it down.
☞ Move the cursor slowly upwards. You will see that the further you go, the more rounded the head becomes. And if you move downwards again, the head becomes more square again.

Release the mouse button when the head looks something like our example on the previous page.

And now a good strong skull in case of accidents

You can also **select** using the Shape tool. This time the Shape tool provides fewer possibilities than the Pick tool. But you can give a line a different thickness by means of the Shape tool.

- ☞ While the Shape tool is still active and the head is selected, click on the **Outline tool**.
- ☞ Click on the line which next to thickest.

Making the entire head bigger

Someone called you a bighead at school today. Having looked in the mirror, you decide that there may be a grain of truth there.

- ☞ Select the entire head by dragging a frame around it using the Pick tool. For a change, you could click on the **Select All** option from the **Edit** menu if you like.
- ☞ Move the head a little to the left and then drag the lower right-hand corner downwards to the right.

In this way, you can see that moving and stretching (and also other manoeuvres with the Pick tool) can take effect on a number of selected components.

A stack of sheets

We have already mentioned that the components which we have drawn lie 'loosely' on the page. Each component you draw seems to lie on a very thin sheet which is laid across the previously drawn component. The figure below illustrates what is meant:

Sheet 1 is completely at the bottom, sheet 2 is on top of this and sheet 3 is at the top.

We can illustrate this in the self-portrait using yet another selection method.

- ☞ Select the head using the **Pick tool**.
- ☞ Press the **Tab** key. Now the tooth is selected. The head was the last component you drew. Before that you drew the tooth. If you press the Tab key again, the mouth should be selected.
- ☞ Press the **Tab** key several times.

You see that the mouth, the left pupil, the right pupil, the left eye etc. are selected one by one, in exactly the reverse order of sequence in which you drew them. You move through all the sheets in the stack as it were. If you press **Shift-Tab** you reverse the order again. You can continue pressing Tab; you will eventually come round to the head again.

By the way: these sheets have nothing to do with the 'Layer' which appears on the status bar sometimes. This 'Layer' is not really important at the moment.

You can move a sheet upwards or downwards in the stack. This can be very useful as we shall now show. We are going to colour in the self-portrait.

Colouring in

☞ Select the head alone (the skull).
☞ Click on a not-too-dark colour in the colour palette.

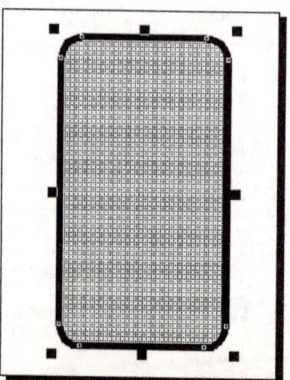

Colouring in

Hey, what's going on? We have filled in the head. Because the head was the last component we drew, it is right at the top of the stack. And accordingly, it covers all the other components. Fortunately, we can change this state of affairs quite easily.

☞ Click on the **Arrange** menu on the menu bar. The following menu appears:

```
Arrange
Layers Roll-Up...    Ctrl+1
Align...             Ctrl+A

To Front             Shift+PgUp
To Back              Shift+PgDn
Forward One          PgUp
Back One             PgDn
Reverse Order

Group                Ctrl+G
Ungroup              Ctrl+U

Combine              Ctrl+C
Break Apart          Ctrl+K

Separate
Convert To Curves    Ctrl+V
```

☞ Click on the **Back One** option. You can also press the **PgDn** (PageDown) key.

We have **not** selected the selection as we did with the Tab key. The skull is still selected. We have placed the sheet containing the skull **under** the sheet containing the tooth.

☞ Press **PgDn**. Now you see not only the tooth but also the mouth:

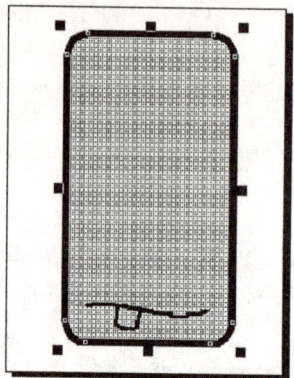

☞ Press the **PgDn** key another five times.

The skull has been moved right to the bottom. You could also have done this by pressing **Shift-PgDn**. If you open the **Arrange** menu again, you can see which keys you can use for these functions.

We shall now colour in the rest of the face.

☞ Select an eye and choose the white box in the colour palette. Do the same with the other eye.

Have you noticed that the colouring information is also shown on the status bar? When you have selected a component, information is shown here, such as **Fill: White** or **20% Black** or **Electric Blue**.

 Removing the colour filling

If you wish to remove a colour filling, select the component in question and then click on the diagonal cross at the extreme left of the colour palette.

Many more colours

The colour palette also has scroll bars. If you click on these, the palette will shift. There are thus many more colours available than you first imagined.

We can't fill this tooth

It would be ideal if we could make this tooth gleaming white as well, but that is very difficult. Unfortunately the tooth does not form a **closed path** as one says. The tooth looks like this:

It is not possible just to pour some white in. Corel-DRAW does not work in that way. You cannot fill a component which is not closed. Sad but true. We must remember this for the next drawing.

Let's do the nose

- ☞ Select the nose.
- ☞ Click on the **Fill tool** in the toolbox. A (different) pop-up menu appears similar to that when you clicked on the Outline tool.

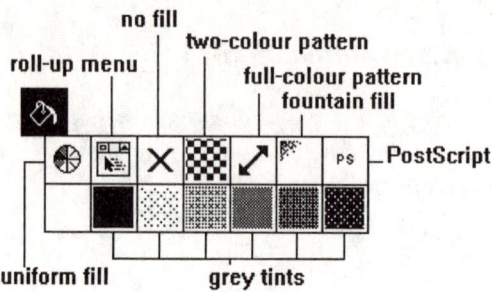

You will see that you can also choose white, black and several grey tints here. There are also a number of other possibilities which we shall deal with. The option we now wish to use is a **fountain fill**.

☞ Click on the **fountain fill** box. That is the box next to the one containing PS. The following window appears:

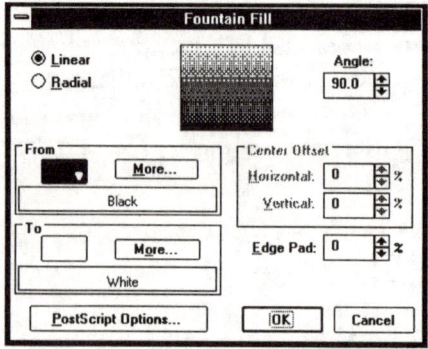

A sample of this filling is shown under the title bar in the **Fountain Fill** box. There is white at the top and black at the bottom and the filling ranges gradually from one to the other.

Let's do the nose 57

In the top left-hand section of the box, you may choose between **Linear** and **Radial**.

☞ Click on the button in front of **Radial**.

The example in the sample box changes. The filling no longer gradually changes from top down to bottom; it changes from outside to centre.

We shall alter the colour filling to produce a more attractive effect. At the moment the colour ranges from black at the outside to white at the centre. We shall change this to: from a light colour at the outside to black at the centre.

☞ Click on the box under the word **From**.

A colour palette appears.

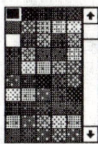

☞ Choose a light colour.
☞ Now click on the box under the word **To**. A colour palette appears here too. Choose black.

The sample box should now look like this:

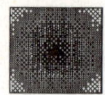

The black spot is exactly in the middle. But it would be better for our nose if it were a little lower down. Fortunately we can shift it quite easily:

☞ Place the cursor on the sample box. The cursor becomes a cross.
☞ Place the cursor a little below the middle of the box and click.

The window looks something like this after all these activities. You may have chosen a different light colour than we have; this is not important.

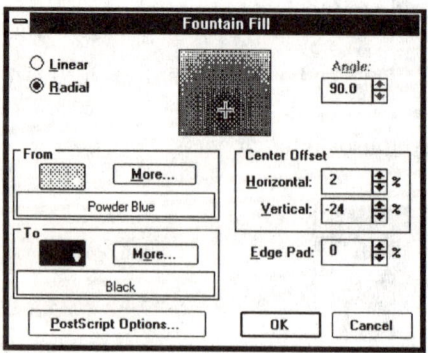

☞ Click on **OK**.
☞ Press **Esc** to make sure that the nose is no longer selected.

The self-portrait is a real work of art. Pity about the tooth though.

Let's do the nose 59

 F9

*If you want to see your drawing without any CorelDRAW extras around it, press **F9**. The drawing is then displayed as it would be when printed. If you want to return to the normal screen, press **Esc** (or any other key).*

 Wireframe

*If you find that it takes too long before the drawing is reconstructed after you have had a menu window on your screen for instance, you can press **Shift-F9**. (Or you can select the **Edit Wireframe** option from the **Display** menu.) In that case, you work further with a wireframe model in the normal screen. The colours are not lost, they are just not shown. When you work like this, all the changes which you make are applied much quicker. All relevant information about line thickness, colour etc. is still shown on the status bar. If you press Shift-F9 again, the whole drawing is displayed once more. While you are*

> working with the wireframe, you can always have a quick look at the drawing by pressing F9.

Smelling round the corner

We shall now turn the nose on the self-portrait.

Perhaps you have unintentionally clicked twice on a line or area in your drawing when selecting it? In that case, instead of the familiar black blocks, you will have produced sets of arrows like these:

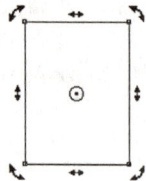

If you click on something that is already selected, you can do other things using the Pick tool: **rotate** and **skew**.

We want to turn the nose as we mentioned. In order to work a little faster on the screen, we shall now use the wireframe.

- ☞ Press **Shift-F9**.
- ☞ Select the nose.
- ☞ Click again on the nose. The nose now looks like this:

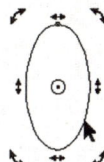

☞ Click on one of the curved arrows at the 'corners' and hold down the mouse button. The cursor changes into a cross.

☞ Move the cursor upwards a little. The cursor again changes shape. You will notice that you can turn the nose.

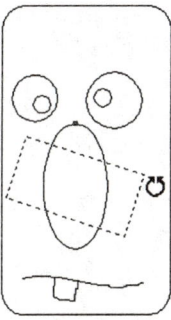

☞ Turn the nose a couple of times and release the mouse button when the nose is roughly as it was in the beginning.

There is a small circle with a dot in the middle of the nose. This is the point around which the nose was turned a moment ago. This is the object's centre of rotation. You can move this centre to another position if you wish.

☞ Click on the centre, hold down the mouse button and move the dot upwards:

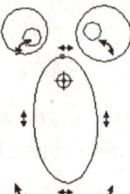

☞ Release the mouse button.
☞ Click on one of the curved arrows and turn the nose again.
☞ Release the mouse button when the nose is approximately in this position:

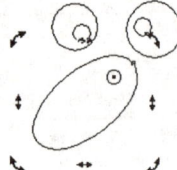

☞ Press **Esc**. Switch off the wireframe by pressing **Shift-F9**.

We have now completed our masterpiece. If you now print it, you will notice that it takes much longer than it did the first time. This is due to the thicker lines and the filling colours.

Smelling round the corner

Saving the portrait under a new name

We shall save our portrait under a different name. This can be useful since we then keep the first version; in other words, it is not **overwritten**.

☞ Select the **Save As** option from the **File** menu. The **Save Drawing** dialog box appears. The name **selfport.cdr** is already filled in:

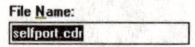

☞ Press the **Backspace** key and type the name: **colport**.
☞ Press the key combination **Alt-F4** to close down CorelDRAW.

3   An anti-dinosaur poster

After our self-portrait, it's now time for something completely different. Let's make a poster which illustrates that we're **against** dinosaurs. If you're **for** dinosaurs, you can also participate (but may have to adjust your poster to your own ideas).

The poster will certainly not look like this:

The eventual result is shown towards the end of this chapter.

Adjusting CorelDRAW a little

Before beginning with the poster, we must deal with a couple of topics. We shall also adjust a few CorelDRAW **settings**. This is not really necessary in order to create the poster but they are important and do influence your work.

☞ Start CorelDRAW again if you have not already done so.

 Beginning a new drawing

*If you want to begin a new drawing while you are in Corel-DRAW and there is a drawing already on the screen, select **New** from the **File** menu.*

The page settings

The page shown on your screen has a certain height and a certain width. These should correspond (proportionally) to the paper in your printer. In **Windows** the settings will be correct if Windows has been correctly installed to suit your computer and printer, but you might still have to make the correct settings for CorelDRAW. We shall now have a look at the present settings.

☞ Find out the width and height of the paper in your printer. You probably have **A4** paper (210 x 297 mm. or 8.27 x 11.69 in.).

The page settings

☞ Open the **File** menu.

Have you noticed that the name of your self-portrait is shown at the bottom of the menu options? If you click on the name the file will be automatically loaded. But we shall not do that now.

☞ Click on **Page Setup**. The following dialog window appears:

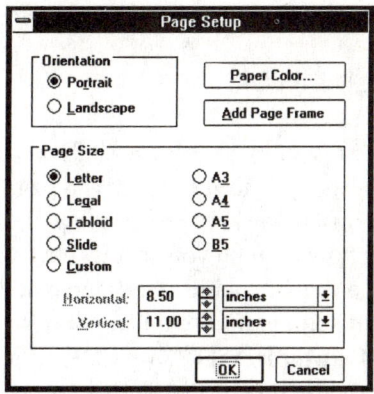

This box enables you to change a number of settings. The most important of these are the **Orientation** and the **Page Size**. We shall not change the first one at the moment. But you should change the paper size to the size that you do actually have in your printer.

☞ Click in the circle which corresponds to the sort of paper you have. (You might have a square instead of a circle; this depends on the type of monitor.)

If you have a paper size which is not shown here, click on **Custom**. Then you can type the size in the Horizontal and Vertical boxes underneath.

You can also change the sizes by clicking on the small arrows at the sides of these boxes.

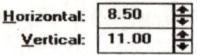

Many menus in CorelDRAW work in the same way.

☞ Click on **OK**.

In the rest of this book, we shall presume that you are working with **A4** paper. The page settings you have just made apply to all drawings you make from now on until you specify new settings. **If you load a drawing which has been made using a different setting,** *that* setting applies from that moment **onwards.** SELFPORT.CDR for instance, has a different setting ('Letter'). This setting is stored along with the drawing and if you load this file, the new setting is lost.

The co-ordinates and the rulers

You have probably noticed that at the left-hand side of the status bar there are all kinds of numbers which change as you move the cursor. These are the **co-ordinates**. These co-ordinates indicate exactly where the cursor is on the page. Move the cursor to the bottom left-hand corner of the page. The status bar then shows the co-ordinates **(0.00, 0.00)**.

The co-ordinates and the rulers 69

This point is thus the 'grid origin' point.

If you want to draw something very precisely, it can be very useful to know the exact cursor position. The **rulers** can also assist you in this task. Rulers look like this:

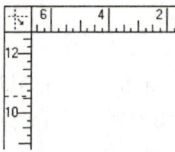

You cannot see them at the moment, but we shall make them visible in the following way:

☞ Click on the **Display** menu on the menu bar. The following menu is opened:

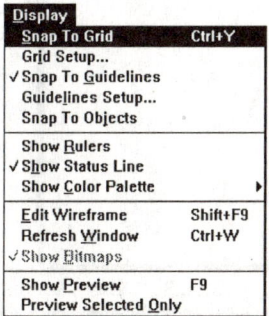

You will see that a tick is shown in front of some of these options. If a tick is shown, it means that the option in question is **active**. If you then click on the option, the tick disappears, meaning that the option has been switched **off**. If you click on it again, the option is switched **on** once more. You will see that there is no tick in front of the **Show Rulers** option, indicating that this option is **off**. You have already become familiar with this principle with the wireframe drawing. The rulers are now to be switched on:

☞ Click on **Show Rulers**.

A tick is placed in front of the option, although you do not see this because the menu disappears immediately. The screen looks like this:

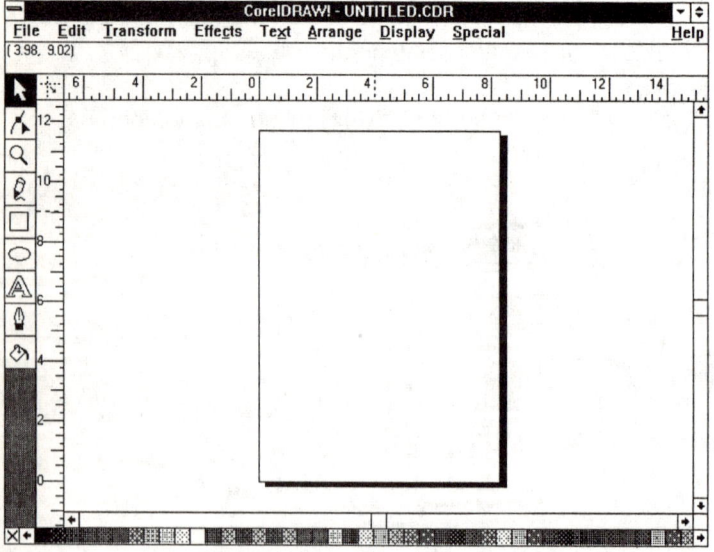

You notice that the rulers are displayed at the top and at the left-hand side of the screen. The measurements of the paper should now correspond to the settings you made in the **Page Setup** window, a little more than 8" wide and just less than 12" in length.

Symbols

CorelDRAW provides many small drawings, **symbols**, which you can use in your drawings. Have a look at the toolbox. The letter **A** represents the **Text tool**. We shall work with text in chapter 6. But this box not only represents the Text tool, it also represents the **Symbols tool**.

☞ Move the mouse pointer to the **Text tool**. Hold down the mouse button for roughly one second. A pop-out menu appears. Release the mouse button.

This menu works a little differently than the Outline tool and the Fill tool menus. You can replace the Text tool with the Symbols tool in the toolbox. We shall now do this.

☞ Click on the box containing the star.

The Symbol tool replaces the Text tool immediately. It will remain there until you move the mouse pointer to that box, hold it down for roughly one second and then click on the Text tool. We shall not do that now.

☞ Click somewhere in the middle of the page. The following window appears on the screen:

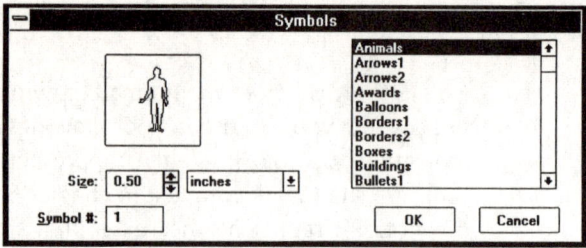

You can choose all kinds of symbols from this window. The symbols are divided into groups, the names of which are shown in the right-hand part of the window.

☞ The **Animals** group is currently selected. In the example box at the left of the window, the first animal is displayed. That is ... a human!

☞ Click in this example box. A drop-down menu opens.

If you click on the scroll bar, many more animals will be displayed.

☞ Click twice on the arrow pointing downwards in the scroll bar. A number of prehistoric animals appear.

☞ Click on the dinosaur second from the left. The drop-down menu closes. The dinosaur is shown in the example box.
☞ Click on **OK**.

Weren't dinosaurs quite large?

Indeed, the symbol is rather small. But fortunately we can do something about it just like any other object. It is regarded as being a **curve**, as the status bar indicates.

☞ Click on the **Pick tool**. The dinosaur is selected (it was already selected, but you could not see that clearly):

☞ Now enlarge it considerably (by placing the cursor on the right-hand corner, holding down the mouse button and moving the cursor upwards to the right) and place it in the middle of the page by clicking on the node and dragging it. Now colour in the dinosaur using black. It will look like this:

 Selecting a filled object

*If an object is filled, you do not have to click on the outline to select it, or to move it once it has been selected. You only need to click anywhere **in** the object.*

Grab the magnifying glass

We shall now see what we can do with the **Zoom tool**.

☞ Click on the **Zoom tool**. A pop-out menu appears:

Grab the magnifying glass

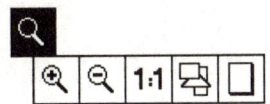

Zooming in

☞ Click on the magnifying glass with the + and move the cursor to the right. As soon as the cursor enters the work area, it changes into a magnifying glass with a + in it.

☞ Click somewhere in the middle of the dinosaur. See what happens? You have now zoomed in **once** which means that everything is now twice as large. That is shown not only on the dinosaur itself but also on the ruler.

☞ Do the same another two times.

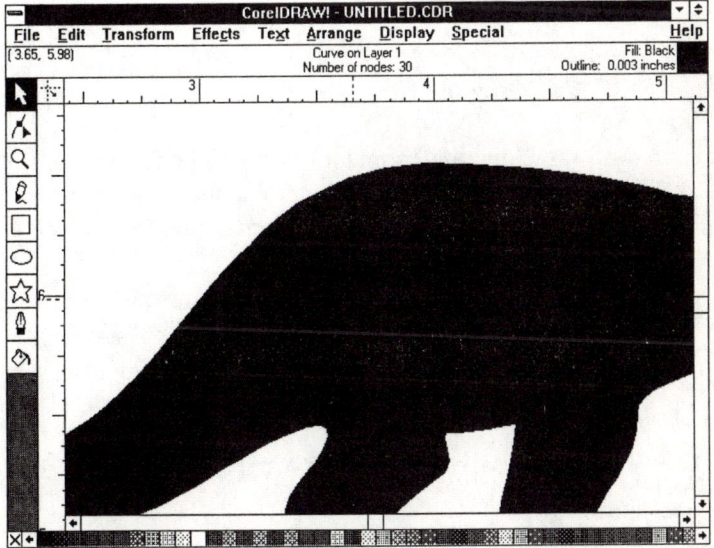

Zooming in using F2

Instead of clicking on the Zoom tool and then on the magnifying glass with the plus, you can simply press the F2 function key. The cursor is then immediately changed to the magnifying glass with the plus sign.

When you have zoomed in, you can still carry out all kinds of jobs. You may think that is not so because you cannot see the black selection boxes (they are now offscreen). Nevertheless all the tools remain available for use.

If would be very inconvenient if you could zoom **in** but could not zoom **out** again. Fortunately, you can do both.

Zooming out

☞ Open the Zoom tool menu and click on the magnifying glass containing the minus sign (-). If you prefer, you can click on the **F3** function key instead.

Now you do not need to click anywhere using the cursor since zooming out takes place from the middle of the picture.

☞ Zoom out once more (use **F3** since it is quicker).

So, now we have the dinosaur. Now we have to

think up a way of showing that we are **anti**-dinosaurs. We could draw a heavy cross through the dinosaur; but maybe we can do it in a more subtle way.

A kick on the behind

We shall use a different symbol.

☞ Click on the **Symbol** tool and then on the position on the figure below where the cross is shown.

The Symbols dialog box appears.

☞ Click on the scroll arrow in the list of symbols.
☞ Click on **SportsFigures**.

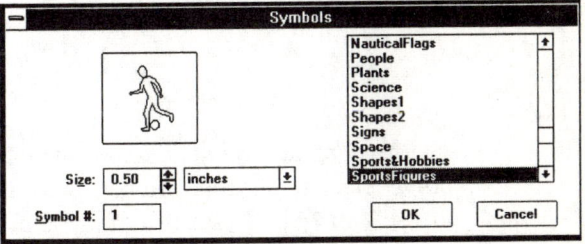

The first figure (the footballer) will do. We cannot use it in its present form but we can alter it quite easily to suit our wishes.

☞ Click on **OK**.

We shall zoom in again in a moment. But we shall first do something which makes zooming in even easier.

☞ Click on **Special** on the menu bar.
☞ Select the **Preferences** option.
☞ Click on the button showing **Mouse**.
☞ Click on the button for **2x zoom** and then on **OK**.

Now you can always zoom in by clicking on the **right** mouse button. This is very handy.

☞ Click on **OK** again to leave the dialog box.

We shall now zoom in on the footballer.

☞ Click twice on the footballer using the **right** mouse button.

The small nodes on the lines indicate that the symbol is selected (because you have just placed it there). You will also see that the symbol consists of three components: a head, a body and a ball. All three are selected.

A kick on the behind

☞ Click on the **Pick tool**. The familiar black blocks appear. These also indicate that all three objects are selected.

☞ Press **Esc** to undo the selection and then try to select the head **alone**.

As you see, you will not succeed! But why not? It is clear that there are three separate objects. But the status bar states that it is a **curve** and not **three selected objects**. All very strange.

The solution is quite straightforward. The three objects are **combined** to form one object, even if they are not made up of one and the same curve. We shall change this.

☞ Click on **Arrange** on the menu bar.

The menu shows a number of options, including **Combine** and **Break Apart**. You cannot choose the first of these because the objects are already combined.

Arrange	
Layers Roll-Up...	**Ctrl+1**
Align...	Ctrl+A
To Front	Shift+PgUp
To Back	Shift+PgDn
Forward One	PgUp
Back One	PgDn
Reverse Order	
Group	Ctrl+G
Ungroup	Ctrl+U
Combine	Ctrl+C
Break Apart	Ctrl+K
Separate	
Convert To Curves	Ctrl+V

☞ Click on **Break Apart**.

The status bar now indicates that something has happened. It shows: **3 objects selected on Layer 1**.

☞ Press **Esc** and select the football alone. This time you will succeed!
☞ Press **Delete** to remove the ball.

Select the footballer by dragging a frame around him. You cannot select the whole figure by clicking on it because you have just split it into separate parts.

We shall now rotate the figure a little.

☞ Click on the outline of the footballer. Arrows appear, replacing the blocks.

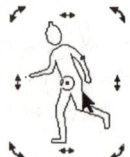

☞ Rotate the figure a little, as shown below. (Remember how this is done? Place the cursor on one of the curved arrows at the corners, press the left mouse button and hold it down. Move the cursor and then release it at the proper moment.)

Mirror image

☞ Press **Esc** and then **F3** twice to zoom out.

This is the result:

Of course, our poster is not finished. The footballer has to chase the dinosaur away. We shall begin by turning the dinosaur around.

Mirror image

☞ Select the dinosaur.
☞ Click on the **Transform** menu. The following options are shown:

Almost everything that you can do with this menu can also be done using the cursor (when the object is selected). But these options enable you to work much more precisely.

☞ Click on **Stretch & Mirror**. A dialog box appears:

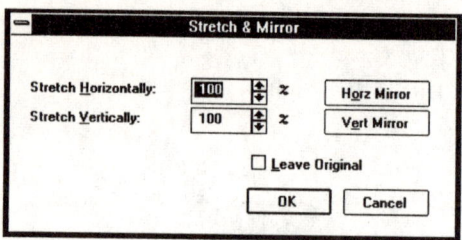

The **Stretch Horizontally** and **Stretch Vertically** options correspond to stretching the object using the cursor and selection blocks which we have already dealt with. In this box, you can enter exact how much stretching or shrinking should occur.

We are going to use the **Horizontal Mirror** function.

☞ Click on the **Horz Mirror** button. You will see that the number in the **Stretch Horizontally** box changes to **-100**. This means that the object will not be stretched or shrunk. It will only be mirrored. (An object can be squeezed to 0 and then enlarged to 100% again on the other side as it were.)
☞ Click on **OK**.

The dinosaur has now been mirrored.

Mirror image

 Mirroring using the Ctrl key.

*You can also mirror an object using the cursor. Select the object, press the **Ctrl** key and hold it down. Place the cursor on one of the small black blocks, press the left mouse button and hold it down. Then move the cursor in the direction in which you want the object to be mirrored. A frame appears. When you cross the edge of the object, the frame turns. When you release the cursor, the object is mirrored.*

We now wish to enlarge the footballer. First we should combine the head and body to form one object.

- Drag a frame around the footballer.
- Click on the **Arrange** menu.
- Click on **Combine**.

The footballer is united again. The status bar also indicates this: **Curve on Layer 1**.

- Now enlarge the footballer and fill him in with black.

We shall now create the effect of movement.

- Give the dinosaur a grey filling, move it a little and rotate it a small amount as shown in the following figure.

☞ Select the dinosaur if it is not already selected.

Copying the dinosaur

We shall create a **duplicate** of the dinosaur. This means that we are going to place a copy of the object next to the object. You might remember this from chapter 1.

☞ Press **Ctrl-D**.

And there is the duplicate!

Copying the dinosaur

T Where is the duplicate to be placed?

*You can determine **where** a duplicate is to be placed (in relation to the original). This is done in the **Preferences** box which can be opened by clicking on the **Special** menu and then on **Preferences**. The dialog window contains this section:*

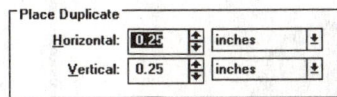

You can specify here where the duplicate should be placed in relation to the original.

> ### Duplicating using the plus key
>
> *You can also make a duplicate in another way. Select the object to be duplicated and drag it to the place where you want to have the duplicate. Do **not** release the mouse button yet. When you are at the proper position press the **plus** key in the numeric keypad at the extreme right-hand side of the keyboard **before releasing the mouse button**.*
>
> *If you select an object and then press the plus key without moving the object, a copy of the object is placed exactly **on top** of the original.*

☞ Now select the second dinosaur, move it to the left and make it a bit smaller. Rotate it a little. Give it a lighter shade of grey.

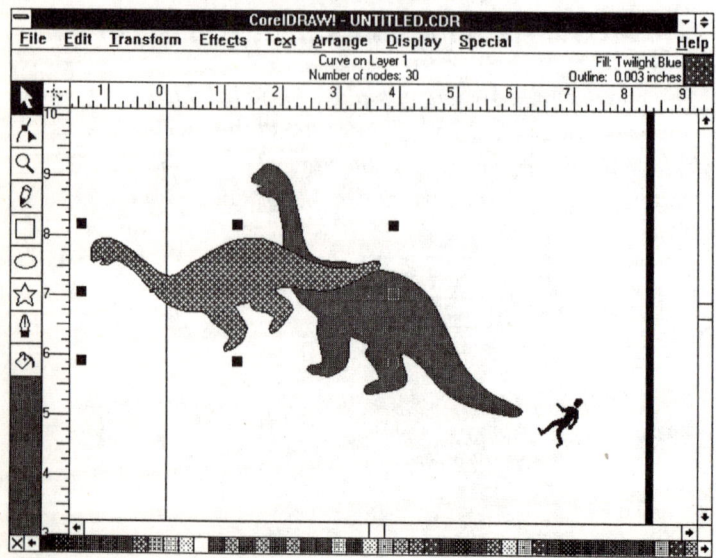

Copying the dinosaur 87

If in your example, the dinosaur moves off the edge of the paper, that is not important. You can just continue working. We shall arrange everything on the page shortly.

 Placing objects next to the page

If you want to remove a part of your drawing but want to keep it just in case you can use it later, you should place it next to the page. It's like placing it on the substitutes' bench. Only what is on the screen page is actually printed out (if the page setup corresponds to the paper in your printer - we discussed this at the beginning of this chapter).

☞ Make a duplicate of this duplicate. Make it a bit smaller, move it, rotate it and give it an even lighter tint. Repeat this process once more.

If you can't keep everything visible on the screen, click on the Zoom tool and click on this symbol in the pop-out menu:

This has the effect that CorelDRAW zooms in or out just far enough to bring everything which belongs to the drawing into view. Pressing **F4** will produce the same result.

☞ Press **F9**. The screen should look like this:

☞ Now press **Esc**.

We shall draw some lines to indicate movement just as real cartoonists do.

☞ Select the **Pencil tool**.
☞ Add some lines around the figures to suggest movement.

Into the rubbish bin

The effect is fine but one important component is still missing: the rubbish bin. That symbol can also be found in CorelDRAW.

Into the rubbish bin

☞ Click on the **Symbol tool** and then under the head of the dinosaur at the extreme left.
☞ Select the **Tools** group from the list of symbols.

You can now click on the hammer and search for a rubbish bin. But you can also enter the number of the required symbol in the Symbol # box. You can find out which numbers belong to which symbols by looking in the book which is supplied along with CorelDRAW: the list of symbols and drawings. The number we are looking for is number **27**.

☞ Click in the **Symbol #** box just behind the 1 and then press **Backspace**. Now type **27**. The rubbish bin appears immediately in the example box.

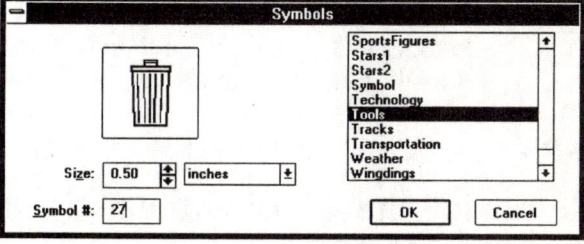

☞ Click on **OK**.
☞ Click twice using the right mouse button on the rubbish bin which has appeared in the drawing.
☞ Enlarge the rubbish bin a little and move it so that the neck and head of the dinosaur fit into it.

90 *An anti-dinosaur poster*

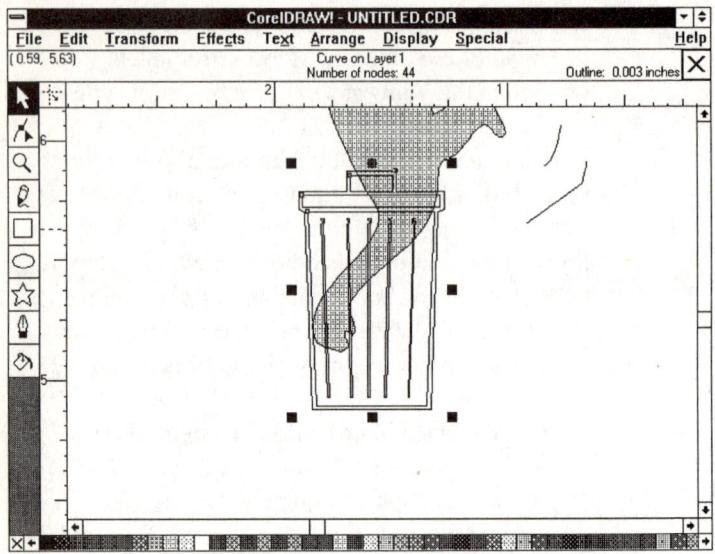

Now we have to do two things. We have to remove the lid of the bin and we have to make sure the bin is not transparent.

Removing the lid using the Shape tool

We shall first remove the lid. The symbol has to be broken apart if we want to get rid of a piece of it.

☞ Make sure the rubbish bin is selected and then open the **Arrange** menu.
☞ Click on **Break Apart**.
☞ Zoom in on the lid using the right mouse button.

Removing the lid using the Shape tool 91

It is quite difficult to remove the entire lid in this drawing because it is not a loose component. We can remove the **handle** quite easily. Then it will look like a bin without a lid.

☞ Click on **Esc** and then select the inner rectangle of the handle.

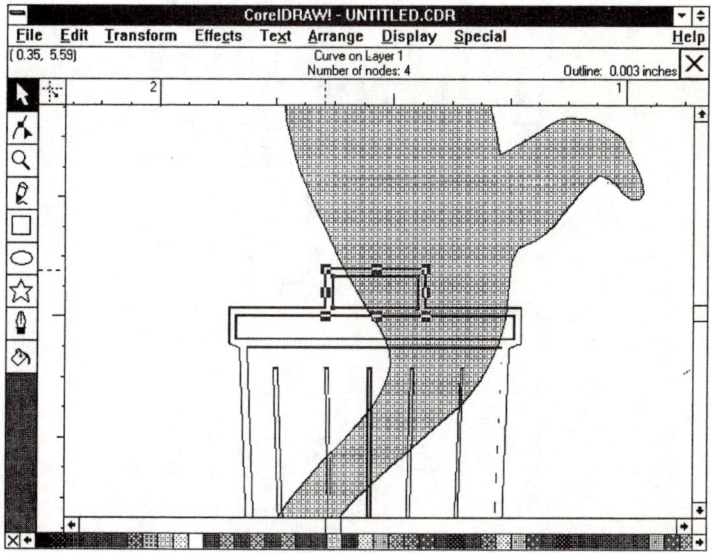

☞ Then press **Delete**.

Now we have to straighten the top line. That is this line (we have omitted the background to make it clearer).

That can be done quite easily using the Shape tool.

☞ Select the top line of the lid and click on the **Shape tool**.

The status bar says: **Curve: 12 nodes**. These nodes are clearly shown as small squares.

☞ Double click on this node:

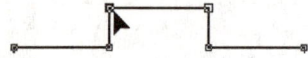

A window appears:

```
┌─ Node Edit ──────┐
│ Delete │   Add   │
│ Break  │   Join  │
│ toLine │ toCurve │
│ Cusp   │ Smooth  │
│ Align… │ Symmet  │
│     Cancel       │
└──────────────────┘
```

This menu enables you to **edit** a node. You can move this window, just like other windows in Windows programs, by clicking on the title bar of this window, holding down the mouse button, moving the cursor and then releasing the mouse button. This is useful if the menu is in the way.

☞ Click on **Delete**.

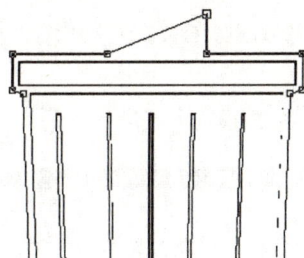

You will see that the node has been removed. The line now runs between the two 'neighbouring' nodes.

☞ Now double click on this node:

Click on **Delete** again in the **Node Edit** menu.

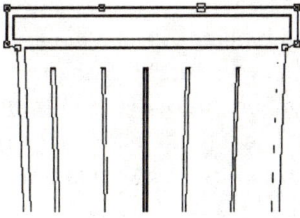

Exactly what we wanted. This is thus one of the functions you can carry out using the Shape tool. Take a quick look at the status bar: **Curve: 10 nodes**.

94 *An anti-dinosaur poster*

Making the rubbish bin opaque

The screen now looks like this:

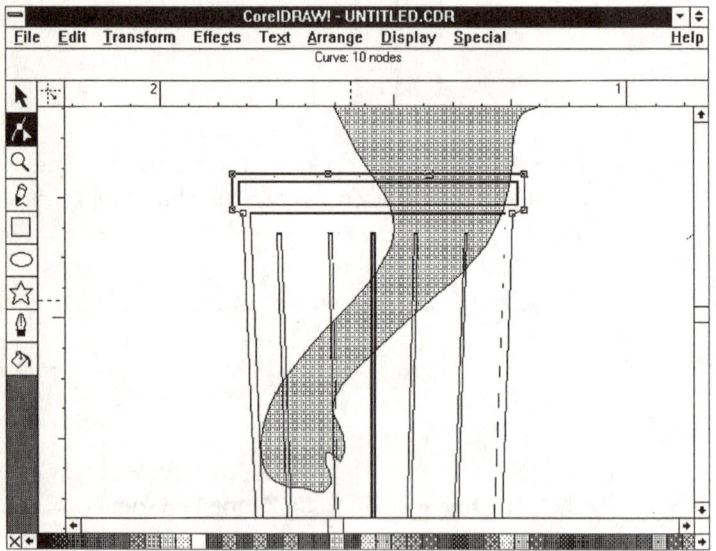

The rubbish bin consists of a number of different objects. Select the **Pick tool** and try to click on the various components of the rubbish bin. It will probably be sufficient to fill in the outer curve (from which we have just removed the two nodes) with white.

☞ Select the outer curve and fill it in using white.

This is the result:

Making the rubbish bin opaque 95

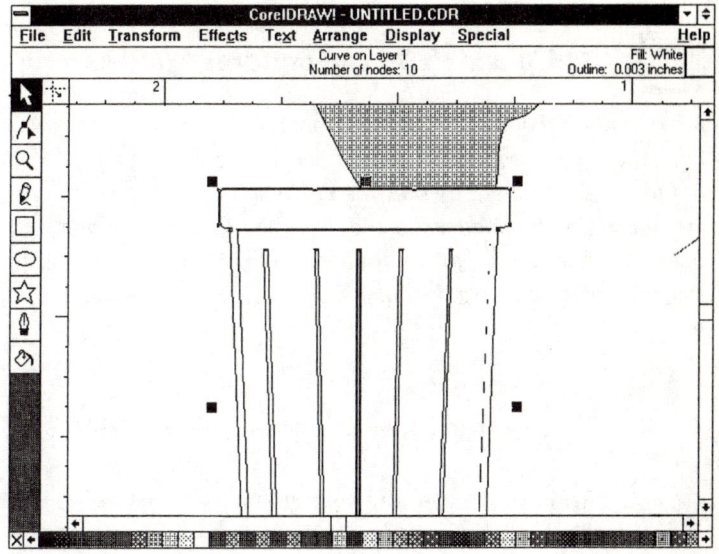

This looks alright apart from the fact that the inner rectangle in the top section has disappeared. This probably means that it is 'behind' the outer curve which we have just filled with white. We can solve this problem quite easily. We shall move the curve which we have just filled with white one level backwards.

☞ Press **PgDn** (the curve must be selected). The rectangle is now **in front** of the curve which was filled with white, making it visible again:

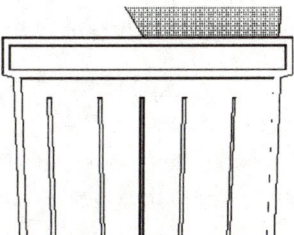

PgUp and PgDn can perform wonders

*Keep in mind that the various components of a drawing are placed on levels on top of one another (even although they do not touch each other). By pressing **PgUp** and **PgDn**, you can move certain components up and down through the drawing levels (in other words, to the front and to the back of the stack). This is often a convenient way of solving filling problems.*

☞ Press **F4** in order to see the complete drawing.

To improve your drawing, you may have to enlarge or decrease the size of the rubbish bin, or to shift it a little. In these cases, select it by dragging a frame around it.

Fitting it all on the page

We now have the small problem that we have gone over the edge of the paper. This will be clear if you zoom out again by pressing **F3** a number of times. This can also be done as follows:

☞ Click on the **Zoom tool** and then on the box at the extreme right of the pop-out menu.

The full page is then shown.

It would be a good idea to turn the drawing so that it fits lengthwise on to the page. To do this, we first

Fitting it all on the page

have to select all the components. This is done by clicking on the **Pick tool** and dragging a frame round the drawing. You can also do so by opening the **Edit** menu and clicking on **Select All**.

☞ Select the entire drawing.

We shall now place the drawing on its side. This can be done by clicking on the drawing once more and turning it using the curved arrows (preferably holding down the **Ctrl** key so that the drawing is rotated in steps). But in this case, we shall use the **Transform** menu.

☞ Open the **Transform** menu on the menu bar.
☞ Click on **Rotate & Skew**. This window appears on the screen:

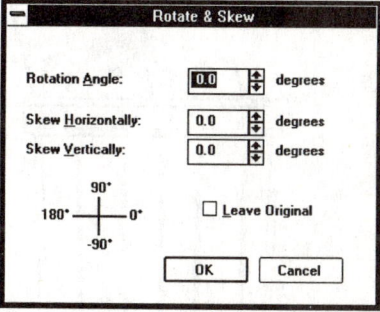

We have to rotate the drawing 90°. You can do that using the arrows, but it is easier just to fill in this number.

☞ Type **90** in the **Rotation Angle** box. Then click on **OK**.
☞ Shift the drawing so that it fits nicely on to the page. Enlarge or reduce it to suit your wishes.
☞ Finally, place a real frame around the drawing using the **Rectangle tool** and make these lines a little thicker.
☞ Save the drawing under the name **nodino**.

The poster is now finally finished. Print it. If you are satisfied, hang it on your wall. If not, make a drawing in which this drawing is confined to the bin!

Fitting it all on the page

4 Break

It's now time to take a break. We shall use that to explain a number of aspects of the program without directly using them to create a drawing. We shall begin drawing again in the next chapter.

It would be useful if you were to experiment with the topics dealt with in this chapter. This will increase your knowledge of the program, and nothing can go wrong. Make sure you begin on an empty page each time (select **New** from the **File** menu). You do not need to save any drawings if you do not like them.

Help!

In CorelDRAW, just as in most Windows programs, you can gain information about the program by pressing **F1** or by clicking on **Help** on the menu bar and then on **Contents**. If you do so, the following window appears:

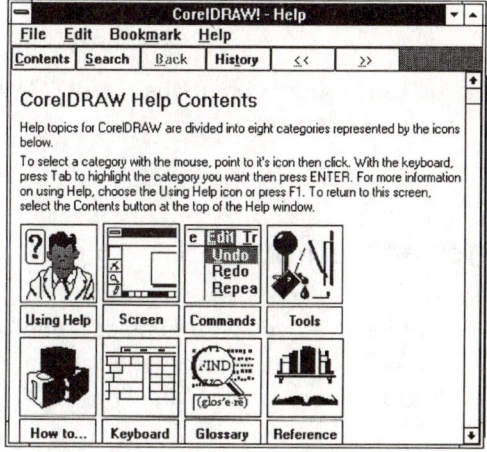

However, it is often not very useful to request help in this way because you don't really know where to begin looking for the relevant topic.

In contrast, the **Shift-F1** key combination can be extremely useful. If you press this combination (the cursor changes into an arrow with a question mark) and then click on a chosen part of the screen, you will get information about the section you clicked on.

If a menu is opened, you can gain information about a certain option by placing the cursor on the option, holding down the mouse button and then pressing **F1**. If a dialog window has been opened, you can just press **F1**. You will then be given information about that particular window.

Keep in mind that the words used in the Corel-DRAW help screens sometimes differ a little from the usage in this book.

You can always return to the CorelDRAW screen by pressing **Alt-F4**.

Gridlines and guidelines

If, for instance, you wish to place a number of figures exactly on one line, you can make use of the **gridlines** and/or the **guidelines**.

Gridlines enable you to work very precisely, especially if the **Snap to Grid** option is activated.

Gridlines

☞ Open the **Display** menu.
☞ Click on **Grid Setup**. The following dialog window appears:

Gridlines and quidelines 103

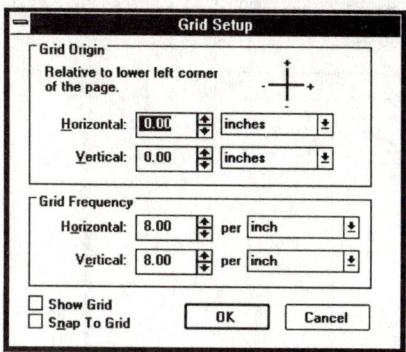

This dialog window enables you to make various settings in the **grid**. The grid is an imaginary sheet of blocked paper lying on top of the page. It can be very useful when you are drawing or when you are moving objects (components).

We shall leave the Grid Origin (the upper section in this window) as it is. The default setting for the grid origin is the bottom left-hand corner of the paper.

But we shall alter the Grid Frequency. This section enables us to change the number of grid lines shown on the page.

☞ Change the values in the **Horizontal** and **Vertical** boxes to **16**.

This dialog box also contains the boxes called **Show Grid** and **Snap to Grid**.

☞ Click on the **Show Grid** and **Snap to Grid** boxes so that both contain a cross.
☞ Click on **OK**.

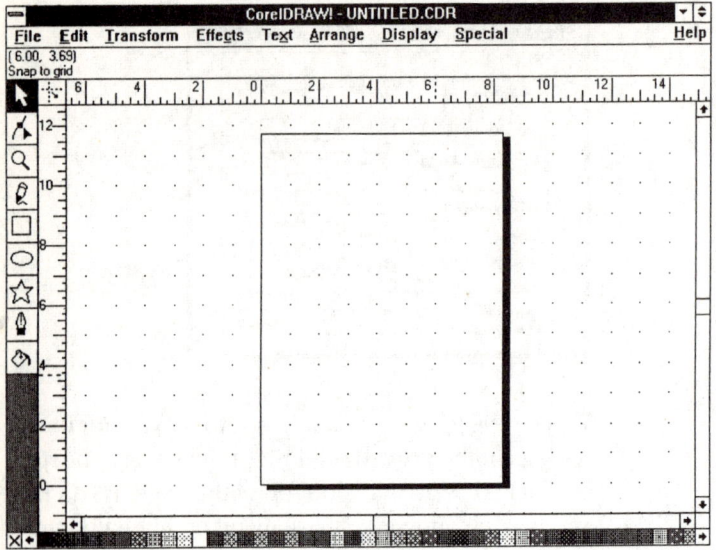

The screen display has been altered. The edit area is covered with dots. This is the grid. But it does not seem to correspond to the settings we made. We specified 16 per inch but much fewer are shown on the screen. This is because otherwise too many dots would be placed on the screen, making it cluttered. The actual amount shown depends on the extent to which you have zoomed in or out. If you zoom in really close you will see that there are indeed 16 dots per inch on the page.

 A looser grid

*If you want a less concentrated grid, you should enter a **smaller** value in the **Grid Frequency** section of the **Grid Setup** box. If you specify for instance **4 per inch**, you will get larger squares. (You can really only see this clearly if you click on the **Zoom tool** to look more closely at the page.)*

The **Snap to Grid** option which you have activated means that when you move figures or components, they are automatically drawn to the nearest gridline, which makes it possible to position them very precisely. For this reason, the fewer gridlines per inch, the larger the steps when moving components when **Snap to Grid** is activated. Try this out. Specify a rather loose grid and then draw a square. When you move it, you will see that this occurs in larger jumps.

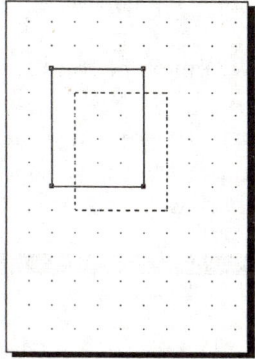

Note: The gridlines setting applies to all subsequent drawing that you make, just like the page settings we deal with earlier. They will only change if you make new settings in the Grid Setup box or if you load a drawing which has been created using other grid settings.

Guidelines

The **Guidelines** function works in much the same way as the **Gridlines** function, except that you determine exactly where the **guideline** is to be positioned. How is this done?

Imagine you wish to place a number of figures on one line.

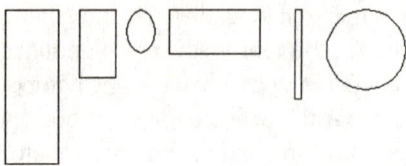

This can be done using the gridlines but it can be done more easily using a guideline.

A guideline is drawn out of the ruler as it were:

☞ Move the cursor to anywhere in the upper ruler. Press the left mouse button and hold it down.
☞ Move the cursor downwards.

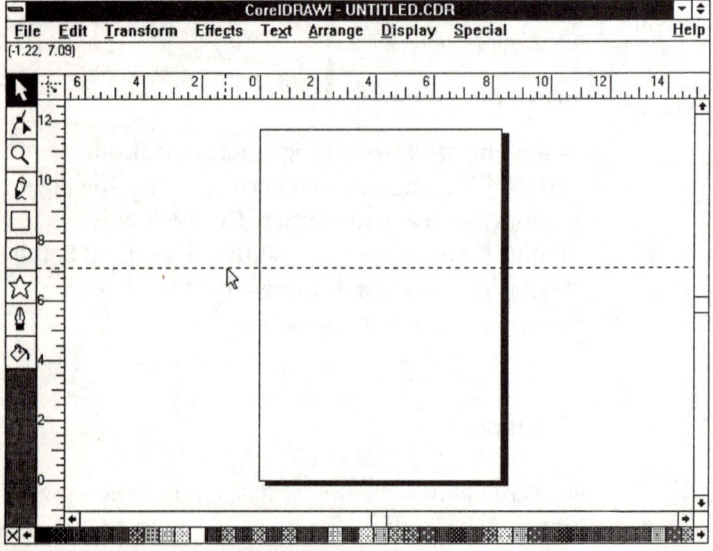

When you release the mouse button, the guideline remains at that position.

☞ Open the **Display** menu. You will see that the **Snap to Guidelines** option is activated (there is a tick mark in front of the option). This indicates that the guideline is automatically 'magnetic'.

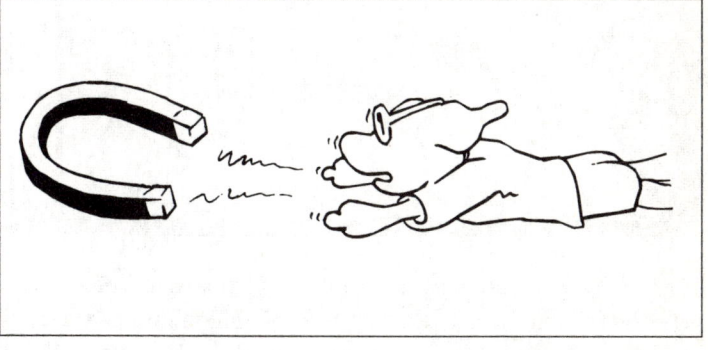

☞ Draw some circles and squares with the upper part somewhere in the vicinity of the guideline.

You will notice that they are attracted to the line. This applies up to a certain distance. Objects placed further from the line will not be attracted; the 'magnetism' is not strong enough. The result is that all objects are positioned neatly on one line.

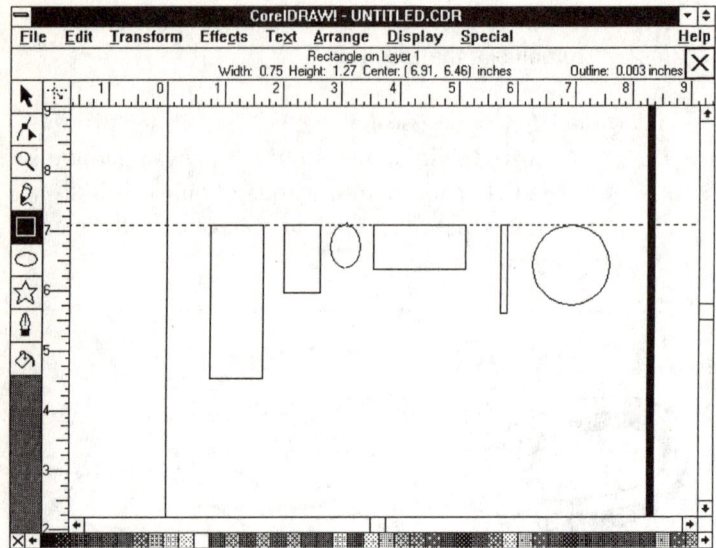

You can activate as many guidelines as you wish, both horizontal and vertical. Guidelines can also be moved by 'picking them up' and setting them down somewhere else. If you no longer need a particular line, pick it up and put it back into the ruler.

You can switch the **Snap to Guidelines** function on and off in the **Display** menu. This menu also provides the **Guidelines Setup** option. This option also enables you to position, move and remove guidelines. However, in practice this is not very handy unless you wish to place a guideline with the utmost precision. We shall not elaborate further on this topic.

Guidelines become linked to the drawing. If you load a different drawing or if you select New from the File menu, all guidelines will disappear. Guidelines are not printed.

Alignment

There is also another way of placing objects neatly under or next to one another. This is as follows:

☞ Place some objects randomly on the page, something like this:

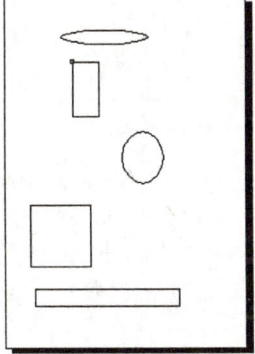

☞ Select all objects (**Edit** menu, **Select All**) and click on **Align** in the **Arrange** menu. The following dialog window appears:

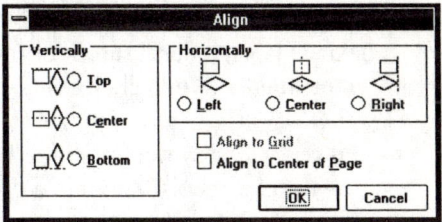

You will see at a glance how these options work. Click on the Center option in the Horizontally section and then on OK.

The result is as follows:

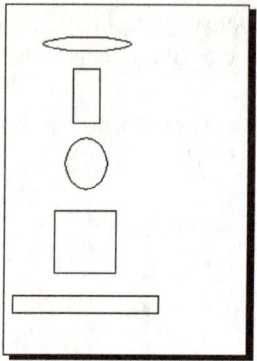

All objects are aligned to correspond with the centre of the object which was last drawn. In our case, that was the flat circle at the top.

The Shift key

You already know that you can select several objects at once using the Shift key, if you cannot or do not want to drag a selection frame across the objects. You can also do something else with the Shift key: you can enlarge, reduce, stretch or squeeze objects **from the middle**. We shall give an example of this:

☞ Place the first symbol from the **Food** group in the list of symbols. Zoom in a couple of times (or press F4).
☞ Press the **Shift** key and hold it down.
☞ Enlarge the symbol by clicking on one of the corner blocks and dragging the mouse.

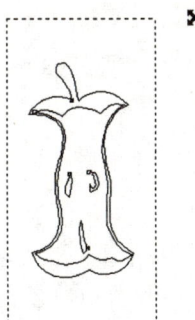

In chapter 6 we shall work with an example which makes good use of this possibility.

You can also perform another action using the Shift key. If you want to place a symbol and you don't want to replace the Text tool with the Symbol tool, Just activate the **Text tool** and then click anywhere on the page **while holding down the Shift key**.

Skew

If you select something and then click on the outline once more, the black blocks turn into curved arrows. These curved arrows enable you to rotate the selected figure. But there are also small straight arrows between the curved arrows:

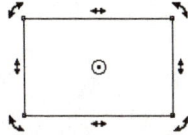

These small straight arrows enable you to slant an object vertically or horizontally:

Just as with rotating, you can also define this very precisely in the **Rotate & Skew** dialog box which appears when you select this option from the **Transform** menu.

Undoing rotation, skewing and mirroring

The **transform** menu also provides the **Clear Transformations** option. When you select an object (or a number of objects) and then click on this option, all rotation, skewing and mirroring which you have applied are undone.

Long live Bézier

We have already practised drawing curved lines a little. You will have noticed that it is not easy to draw a good smooth curve. If you try to draw something like this:

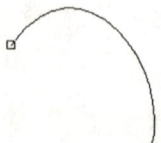

it often becomes something like this:

This is because CorelDRAW follows the movements of your hand exactly. If you tremble just a little, a node is placed and the line is less smooth.

Fortunately, there is another way to draw lines. We shall now try it out.

Curved lines using the Bézier pencil

Remember that we could replace the Text tool with the Symbol tool? In the same way it is possible to replace the Pencil tool with the **Bézier pencil**.

☞ Move the cursor to the **Pencil tool**, press the left mouse button and hold it down for about a second. A pop-out menu appears. Release the mouse button.

☞ Click on the right-hand box.

The Pencil in the toolbox is now replaced by the **Bézier drawing tool**. This tool has this name because you can use it to create so-called **Bézier curves**. You will see this shortly. They are named after a certain Mr Bézier who walked with a stoop (this isn't completely true, but it helps you to remember).

☞ Click on the page where you wish to begin drawing.

You will see that a small black block has been deposited. This is the **node** representing the starting point of the Bézier curve.

☞ Place the cursor on the node, press the left mouse button and hold it down. Move the cursor diagonally upwards.

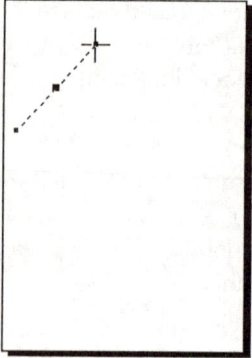

What now appears are the so-called **control points** of the curve. These are handles which enable you to determine just how curved the curve is to be. But of course, it will only be a curve if there is also a finishing point.

Long live Bézier

☞ Click a small distance down and to the right of the starting point. The result is as follows:

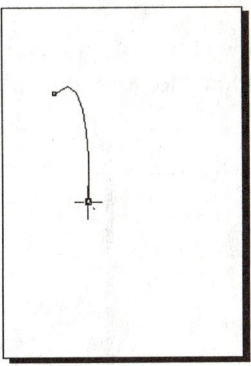

This does not look very special but you would never have been able to make it using the normal Pencil tool. Have a look at the status bar. It shows: **Curve on Layer 1. Number of nodes:2**. The remarkable thing is that there are only 2 nodes, which makes the curve very smooth and which also enables you to alter the extent of the curving. We shall display this:

☞ Click on the **Shape tool**.
☞ Click on the starting node.

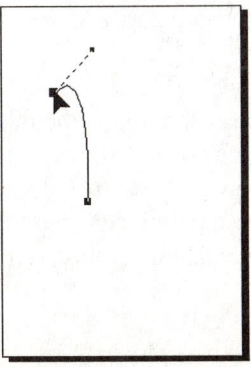

You now see the control point which was placed when you drew the curve. At that time, you moved the cursor upwards to the right.

☞ Click on the control point, hold down the mouse button and move the cursor back and forward.

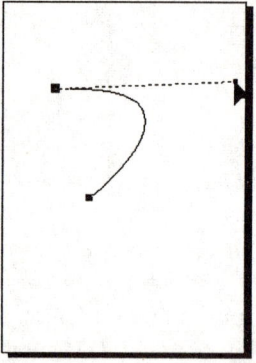

You will begin to realize that this provides fantastic possibilities. But that is not all. We can add a node to the curve.

☞ Double click on the finishing node.

The **Node Edit** menu appears. Select the **Add** option.

A new node has appeared in the middle of the curve. If you click on the starting node, you will see that this new node has **two** control points. This makes it possible to influence the form of the curve even more. An example of this is shown on the next page.

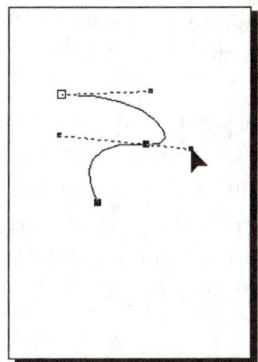

Drawing a straight line with the Bézier tool

Remove the curve by selecting it and pressing **Delete**. We shall now make a straight line.

☞ Select the Bézier drawing tool and click somewhere on the page. Then click on another position on the page.

The status bar states: **Curve on Layer 1**.

☞ Click on the **Shape tool**.
☞ Click on the finishing node.

The status bar now states: **Selected node: Line Cusp**. What's going on here? Is it a curve or is it a line? It all seems rather complicated but in practice it's quite simple: the Bézier tool (and the Pick tool) regard the line as being a curve, but the Shape tool regards it as being a line at this moment. The following procedure shows this:

☞ Click on the starting node and then again on the finishing node.

No control points appear. If you wish to convert this straight line into a curved line, you will have to ensure that control points do appear. In other words, you must make sure that the **Shape tool** regards the line as being a curve. To do this, you have to open the **Node Edit** box.

☞ Double click on the finishing node. You will see that the entire line is selected and that the **Node Edit** menu appears.

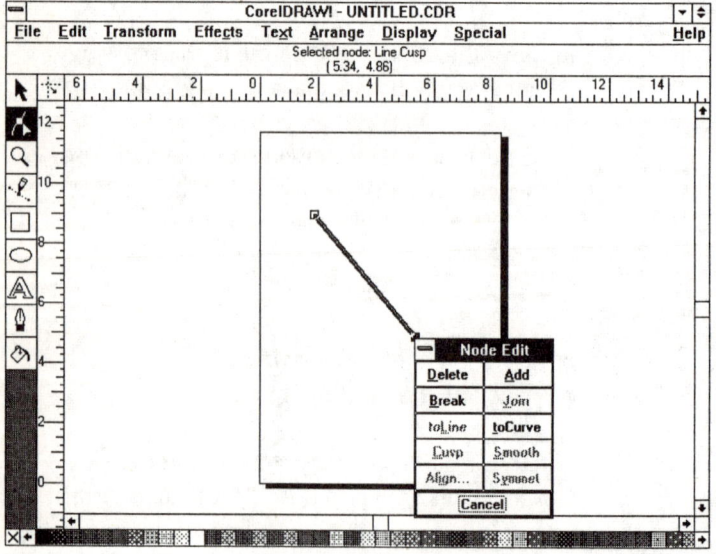

☞ Select **toCurve**. Accordingly, the line is converted to a curve.

The result is a line which does have control points.

The Shape tool now regards it as being a curve. This is also shown on the status bar (**Curve Cusp**). It is now a piece of cake to make it into a smooth curved line:

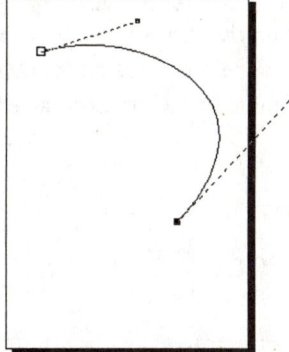

If you have just placed a line or a curve and you want to attach a piece to it, just click somewhere else on the page, as long as the Bézier tool is active. In this way, you can create all the shapes you want:

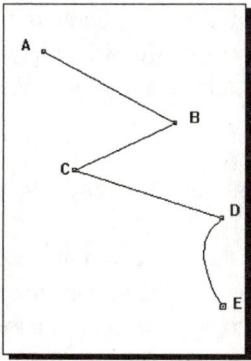

In the lower figure on page 119, we have just clicked on positions A, B, C and D. Then we clicked again on point D and, holding down the mouse button, we drew a dotted line downwards to the left. We released the mouse button and then moved the mouse pointer (the cross) to position E. When we clicked there the curve was formed. The whole shape is regarded as being a curve. That is shown on the status bar: **Curve on Layer 1. Number of nodes: 5**.

More about the Node Edit menu

Objects which you draw using the normal Pencil tool also have nodes. These can be edited by means of the **Node Edit** menu. In this way you can edit **everything** you draw (circles, squares, letters - as we shall discuss shortly). The only thing is that you must always ensure that these objects are regarded as being **curves**.

We have just outlined how to convert a drawn straight line into a curve. But if you have drawn a rectangle, it works a little differently. We shall illustrate this:

☞ Draw a rectangle on an empty page.

If you now activate the Shape tool, you will see four nodes. You can round off the corners using these nodes as we have done previously. But there are no control points. In order to convert a (part of a) rectangle into a curve, you have to do two things:

More about the Node Edit menu 121

☞ Select the rectangle (can also be done using the Shape tool) and open the **Arrange** menu. Then choose **Convert To Curves**.

The status bar indicates that we now have a curve instead of a rectangle. We still have no control points. We can change this by activating the Shape tool and then double clicking on the nodes one by one. The **Node Edit** menu opens each time. Select **toCurve**. The selected section of line is then converted to a curve.

The same effect can be gained in a quicker way:

☞ Ensure that the rectangle has been selected and that the Shape tool is active. Drag a frame around the entire rectangle. If you now double click on any part of the rectangle outline, the **Node Edit** menu appears. The option you now choose applies to **all the nodes** you have selected.
☞ In this case, we want **toCurve**.

If you now click on a node, you will see that control points have been attached. You can now alter the form of each separate line of the rectangle.

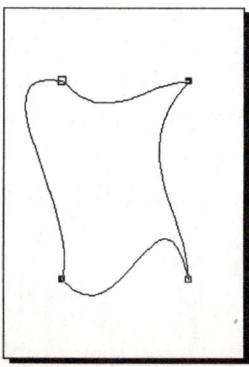

A straight line using the normal Pencil tool

It is easy to draw a straight line using the normal Pencil tool.

- ☞ Activate the **Pencil tool**.
- ☞ Click anywhere on the page.
- ☞ Click at another position on the page.

If you now wish to add an extra line to this line, click next to the end point of the first line and then at another position on the page.

If you join the lines to each other in this way, you will see that the drawing remains one object with a number of nodes.

Converting a curve to a straight line

The **toLine** option from the **Node Edit** menu enables you to convert a curve into a straight line. Imagine that you have drawn this line:

Activate the Shape tool and click on the right node for example. The **Node Edit** menu appears. Select the **toLine** option and this is the result:

More about the Shape tool

Just as with the Pick tool, you can also use the Shape tool to **select** objects (in that case the nodes are shown as transparent small blocks). If an object has been selected (by means of the Shape tool or the Pick tool), you can **activate** the nodes (along with pieces of curves). But it is also possible to activate several nodes at the same time. This provides a number of interesting possibilities.

☞ Place the figure which is symbol # **1** from the Animals group on the screen. Enlarge it until it is clearly visible.

☞ Click on the **Shape tool**. The object was still selected, so all nodes are shown as transparent blocks:

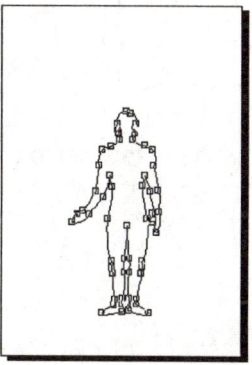

☞ Now activate all nodes by dragging a frame around the symbol. The small blocks all become black.

☞ Double click on one of the lines of the symbol. The familiar **Node Edit** menu opens again.

The command which you now give applies to **all** activated nodes.

☞ Click on **toLine**.
☞ Click on the **Pick tool**. You can now see the figure better. You will notice that all curved lines have become straight.

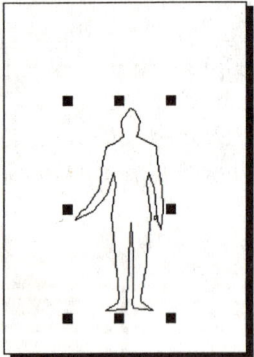

☞ Click on the **Shape tool** again and select the symbol's legs (by means of dragging a box around them) as shown in the figure on the next page.

More about the Shape tool 125

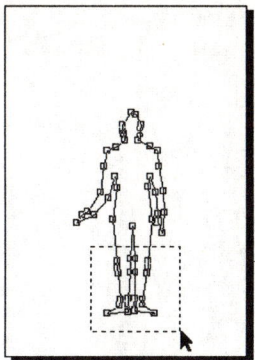

- ☞ Click on one of the activated nodes and hold down the mouse button.
- ☞ Move the cursor. You will see that the legs are pulled in the same direction as the cursor.

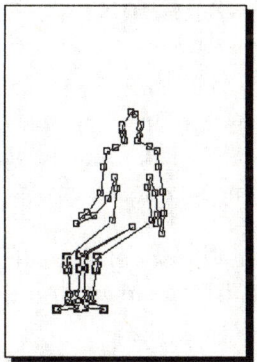

Just as with the Pick tool, you can also use the **Shift** key here:

- ☞ Press the **Shift** key and hold it down.
- ☞ Select several nodes. They do not need to be next to one another.

☞ Release the **Shift** key.
☞ Move the cursor.

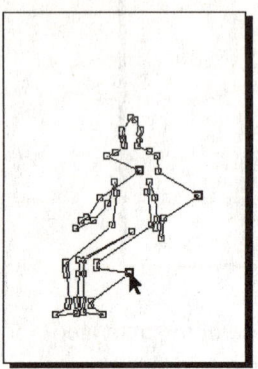

Combining and grouping

We dealt briefly with **combined** objects. The opposite of combining was **breaking apart**. The **Arrange** menu also provides the **Group** and **Ungroup** options. What is the difference between these?

If you **group** two or more objects, they are linked to each other as it were. Imagine you have drawn these two objects:

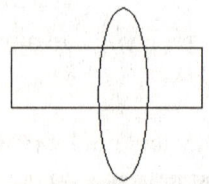

If you now **group** them by selecting both and then choosing **Group** in the **Arrange** menu, you cannot select them individually again. You can only select them together. Actions such as enlarging, rotating, filling etc. are always carried out on **both** objects. But they do remain **individual** objects (as is shown on the status bar). The **Ungroup** option from the **Arrange** menu splits them apart again.

The **Combine** function works a little differently. Two objects are united to form **one curve** (as is also shown on the status bar), even if they do not touch one another. If you then fill in this object (it has become **one** object) something interesting happens: where the overlapping occurs, the background remains visible. You will see something like this:

Importing

Right at the beginning of this book we mentioned that it is possible to gather together all kinds of loose elements or components in CorelDRAW. We have seen a number of examples of this. But the possibilities are very extensive. You can also, for instance, import a drawing or part of a drawing from elsewhere. This may be a CorelDRAW drawing but it may also be a drawing made in Paintbrush for example.

We refer to this as **importing**. This takes place as follows:

☞ Select **Import** from the **File** menu. The following dialog box appears:

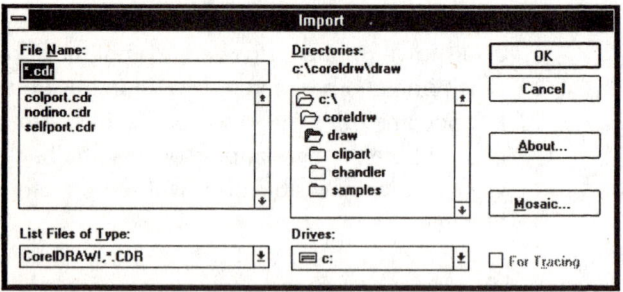

You can now **import** a drawing which already exists. In addition to CorelDRAW drawings (CDR), it is also possible to import all other kinds of files. This can be regulated by clicking on the arrow in the **List Files of Type** box:

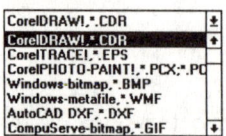

Then select the file which you wish to import and click on **OK**. If it is a CorelDRAW drawing, all objects are automatically grouped in the drawing. If you want to remove or change a part of the drawing, you first have to open the **Arrange** menu and choose the **Ungroup** option.

If you want to import a Paintbrush drawing, choose **Windows Bitmap, *.BMP** from the List Files of Type box in the **Import** dialog window. Then go to the relevant directory and choose the file you want to import. When you have done this, the Paintbrush drawing is displayed but it is not possible to edit it as extensively as a CorelDRAW drawing. A drawing which has been made in Paintbrush and imported into CorelDRAW is shown below.

The status bar shows: **Monochrome Bitmap on Layer 1** (may be Colour Bitmap). When you rotate the drawing, you will see this:

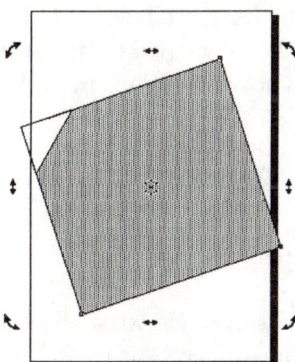

However, the final printout will reproduce it as it should be.

Thus, importing enables you to combine all sorts of things:

The fact that the head is a little ragged is due to the small imperfections in Paintbrush, not in Corel-DRAW. CorelDRAW is really a marvellous program!

On your marks ...!

Now the break is over and we shall continue with a very interesting project.

5 A small correction to the theory of evolution

You have almost certainly heard of the theory of evolution. It is not quite true, as you will see shortly. Assisted by CorelDRAW, we shall prove that humans are not descended from apes but from **donkeys**.

- ☞ Make sure you begin with an empty page.
- ☞ Place a horizontal guideline across the middle of the page.
- ☞ Activate the **Symbol tool** and click at the left-hand side of the page. The **Symbols** dialog box opens. Click on **People** from the list, click on the **Symbol #** box and type **27**.
- ☞ Click on the right-hand side of the page and click on **Business & Government**. Click on the **Symbol #** box and type **59**.

- ☞ Click on **OK**.
- ☞ Enlarge the second symbol a little.
- ☞ Press **F4**.

The screen should look like this:

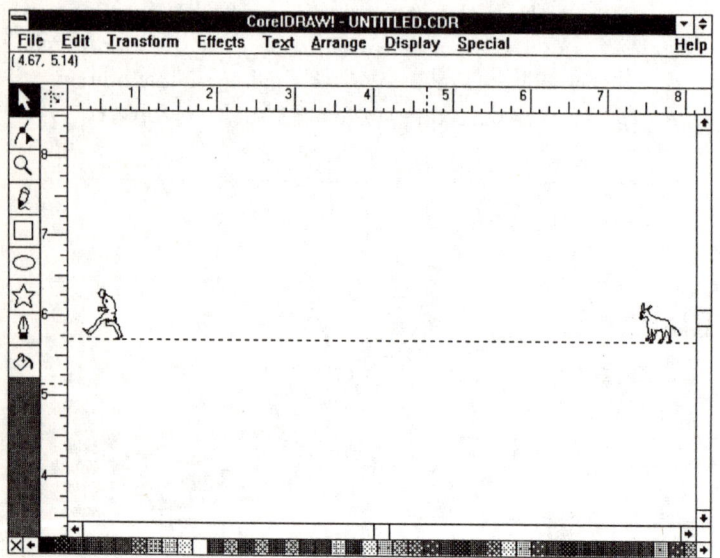

⊤ *Fixing the page*

*If you are working near the edge of the page, it can be irritating if the page keeps shifting offscreen if you move the cursor a little too far to one side. You can keep the page in its place by opening the **Special** menu and choosing **Preferences**. Now remove the cross from the **Auto-Panning** box. Now you will only be able to move the page across the screen by clicking on the scroll arrows at the bottom of the work area.*

We shall now draw a flowing line using the normal pencil, something like this:

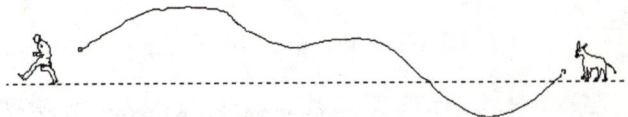

- ☞ Now select both symbols (using the **Shift** key).
- ☞ Fill both objects in with black.
- ☞ Open the **Effects** menu and select the **Blend Roll-Up** option.

Blending

We now get to know a new type of menu, the **roll-up** menu. The **Blend** roll-up menu looks like this:

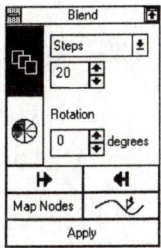

When you place a roll-up menu on the screen, it remains there **until you close it again**. Closing it is done in the same way as closing other windows in Windows applications: double click on the small flat block in the top left-hand corner.

You can also move this menu if you like. That is

also done just as with other Windows windows: click on the title bar and drag the window to the required position.

If you click on the arrow at the top right-hand corner of the box, you will see immediately why this type of menu is called a **roll-up** menu: you can roll the menu up so that it occupies little space on the screen.

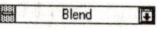

When you want to use it again, just click on the same arrow.

The commands you give using a roll-up menu always only have effect on what you have selected.

- ☞ In the box under **Steps**, change the 20 to **10**.
- ☞ Click on the box showing the arrow and curving line.
- ☞ Then select **New Path**. This is in fact the only possibility available.

When you now bring the cursor out of the roll-up menu, it changes into an arrow with a bent tail.

- ☞ Click on the curved line you drew. Black blocks appear.
- ☞ Then click on **Apply**.

Then something strange and wonderful occurs, as you see.

Blending

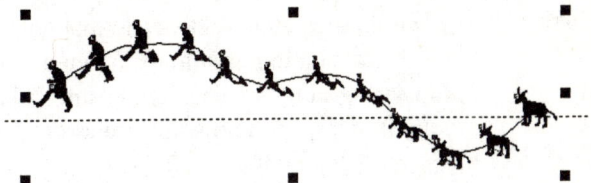

Now we have to remove the **new path** (the curving line we drew). But if you click on the line and press Delete, all the symbols between the human and the donkey will also disappear. We have to go about this in another way.

☞ Open on the **Arrange** menu and click on **Separate**.
☞ Select the line and press **Delete**.

We are almost finished. Since we are used to reading text from left to right, it would also be better if this scientific card of evolution also went in that direction. This can easily be done using the mirroring function as you already know.

☞ Select all the objects and open the **Transform** menu. Choose the **Stretch & Mirror** option.
☞ Click on the **Horz Mirror** box and then on **OK**.

Save the drawing under the name ASSMAN and then print it.

You will immediately understand that you can do a lot of interesting things with this blending function. For instance, you can also blend using colours. Try it out. Here is an example. It is quite simple, you begin with three curves:

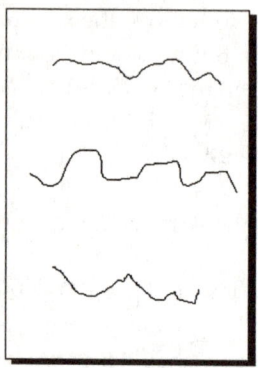

If you now get the first and the second curves to blend into each other, and then the second and third, this will be the result:

6 The microphone

In this chapter we shall create an attractive logo for the school magazine. It is the magazine for St. Michael's School and it's called **The microphone**. What should we place in this logo? The name of the magazine of course, but the headmaster, Mr Gluteus, insists that the name of the school should also appear.

We will use letters for the name of the magazine and of the school. That much is obvious. In CorelDRAW this will be no problem because there are a great deal of letters available, and you can present them in all kinds of attractive ways. Keep in mind that text in CorelDRAW is also treated as an **object**, which means that you can rotate, move, stretch, fill it etc. just as you would do a drawing.

Typing text and choosing the font

☞ Make sure you have an empty page.

When you type text, it automatically gets a black filling (although you can alter this); in addition the letters are given the standard **outline**, which is 0.003 inches in our case. With text it is actually better if there is no outline because if you reduce the size of the letters, the outline can deform them considerably. We shall now determine that the standard setting (also called the default setting) is: **no outline**.

☞ Click on the **Outline tool** and click on the cross in the pop-out menu. The following window appears:

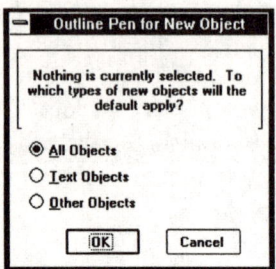

☞ Choose **Text Objects**.

We can now begin.

☞ Click on the **Text tool**. (If the Symbol tool is still visible instead of the Text tool, you will have to activate the Text tool from the pop-out menu. You know how this is done.)
☞ Click on the upper left-hand side of the page and type: **the microphone**.

Typing text and choosing the font 139

You see that the letters appear on the page just as if you were working with a word processor.

☞ Click on the **Pick tool**.
☞ Click twice on the right mouse button.
☞ Enlarge the text until it is roughly as large as shown:

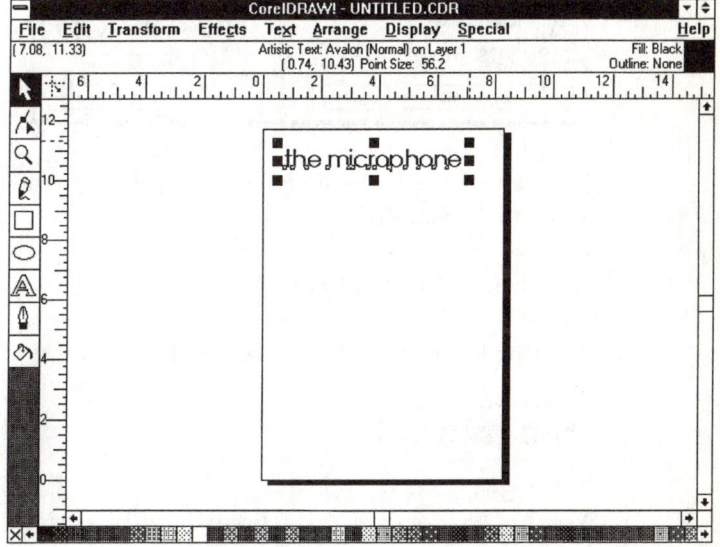

☞ Then click once on the right mouse button while the cursor is approximately in the middle of the text.

The type of letter (referred to as the **font**) which you have automatically used here is called **Avalon**. That is shown on the status bar. It is a bit of a boring font; there's nothing special about it. We shall try a different font.

☞ Press **Ctrl-T**. The following window appears:

[Artistic Text dialog box showing:
- Text field containing "the microphone"
- Fonts list: Aardvark, Arabia, Arial, Avalon (selected), Bahamas, BahamasHeavy, BahamasLight
- Justification: Left (selected), Center, Right, Full, None
- Size: 56.2 points
- Style: Normal
- Sample: "the microp"
- This is a TrueType font.
- Buttons: Spacing..., Import..., Paste, OK, Cancel]

You can choose any one of the dozens of fonts provided in the **Fonts** box.

☞ Click on **BahamasHeavy**.

The sample box at the right shows how that font looks:

the microph

You can browse through the list in this way. Each time you click on a font, the sample box indicates how this font will look. This is **Frankenstein** for instance:

𝔱𝔥𝔢 𝔪𝔦𝔠𝔯𝔬𝔭𝔥𝔬

And this is **TimpaniHeavy**:

the micro

Typing text and choosing the font 141

 Changing text in the Artistic Text box

*You can edit the text in the upper section if that is necessary. As soon as you place the cursor in that box, it changes into a **text cursor**. When you click anywhere in the text, you can then delete, add, change letters etc. You can determine the size of the letters in the **Size** box. Of course, that can also be done just as we have done, by enlarging the text object.*

The font that we wish to use is called **Umbrella**.

☞ Select **Umbrella**. You will see that the letters in the sample box change into capitals. This font, like some others, has only capitals.

☞ Click on **OK**.

The result is shown on the next page.

 You can change the font again and again

*Regardless of how you edit the text objects, in principle you can always change the font when you want. But you cannot do this when you have combined or grouped a text with a different object, or if you have converted the text to curves. As long as the status bar shows that you are working with **text** (if you have selected the text), you are able to change the font.*

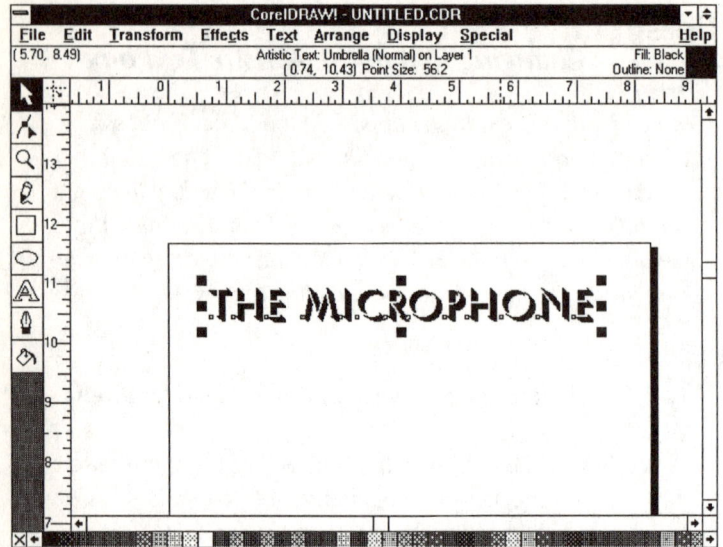

The Text roll-up menu

*Instead of activating the menu you get by pressing **Ctrl-T**, you can also activate a different menu if you want to change the font for example. This is done by pressing **Ctrl-2**. The following roll-up menu appears:*

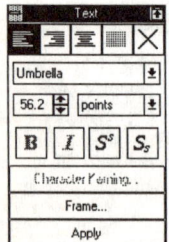

However, this menu provides fewer options than the other text menu.

Perspective

We want to change the form of the text in such a way that it becomes increasingly large from left to right, so that it looks like the word **MICROPHONE** is coming closer. We can easily arrange this with the help of **perspective**.

☞ Make sure that the text is selected.
☞ Open the **Effects** menu and select **Edit Perspective**.

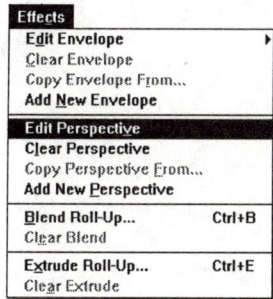

A frame is placed around the text:

THE MICROPHONE

Place the cursor (which now looks a little different) on the top right-hand block of the frame. Press the Left mouse button and drag the block upwards. Then release the mouse button.

In a second or two, CorelDRAW redraws the letters in their new form. In this way, you have changed the **perspective** of the object.

☞ Shift the block in the lower right-hand corner downwards.

The result should look something like this:

See the cross next to the page? This is the so-called 'vanishing point' of this perspective.

☞ Save the logo (just to be safe) under the name **micropho**.

The name of the school

We shall now add the name of the school to the school logo. We shall place that in a circle as you will see.

☞ Draw a circle just under the text (using the **Ctrl** key). The circle should be roughly the same size as the second **O** in MICROPHONE.

The name of the school 145

We now want to place a second circle within this circle, **with the same centre**. This is quite easy as you already know.

☞ Make a copy of the circle at exactly the same place. You only need to select the circle and then press the **plus** key on the numeric keypad at the right of your keyboard. It looks as if nothing has happened but the second circle has been placed precisely on top of the first.
☞ Press the **Shift** key and hold it down.
☞ Click on one of the corner blocks and make the circle smaller. Now you can see that there are two circles. Release the Shift key.
☞ Now select both circles and move them to the position shown in the figure below. The letter **T** should be right in the middle of the circle. Zoom in to get a better view.

We shall now place the name of the school in the circumference of the circle.

- ☞ Click on the **Text tool** and then anywhere under the circle.
- ☞ Type **St. Michael's School**.

You see immediately that the text is much too large. Moreover, it should be in a different font.

- ☞ Press **Ctrl-T**.
- ☞ Choose the **Casablanca** font and change the size to **11** points by clicking on the arrow pointing downwards at the side of the Size box.

We shall now place the text in the circle. That is done by means of the **Fit Text To Path** option from the **Text** menu. When using this option, you need to select two things: the text you want to place on the path, and the path itself. The path may be a line, a square, a circle etc.

In our case, the text is already selected.

- ☞ Press the **Shift** key and select the inner circle. If everything has gone as it should, the status bar should show: **2 objects selected on Layer 1**.
- ☞ Press **Ctrl-F**, which is the same as selecting **Fit Text To Path** from the **Text** menu.

The **Fit Text To Path** roll-up menu appears on the screen.

If the path is an open object (such as a line), the roll-up menu will look a little different. The operation, however, is similar.

☞ Click on the 'nine o'clock' position in the box containing the diagonal cross and the circle. This ensures that the middle of the text will be placed at that position.

☞ Click on **Edit** in the roll-up menu. The following dialog box appears:

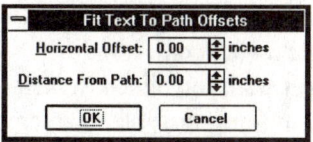

☞ Enter the value 0.05 inches in the Distance From Path section.

☞ Click on **OK** and then on **Apply** in the **Fit Text To Path** dialog box.

Close the roll-up menu by double clicking on the

small button in the top left-hand corner. The result will look like this (after zooming in once more):

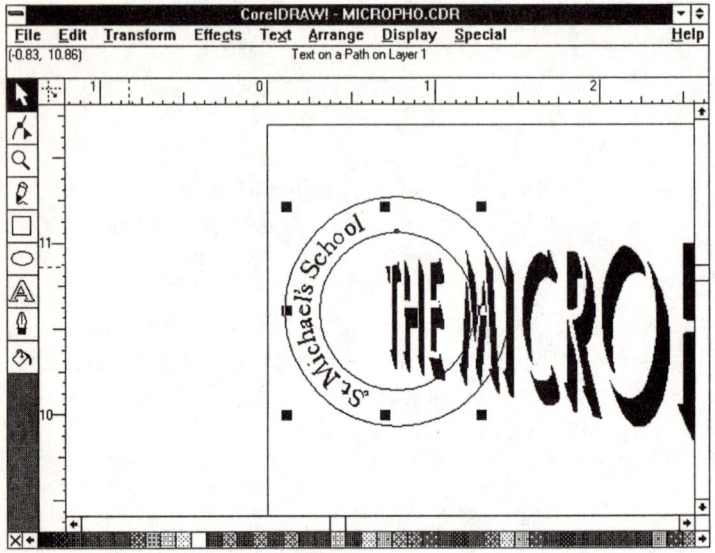

If the letters are too large or small for your liking, proceed as follows:

- ☞ Press **Alt-Backspace**.
- ☞ Select the text only.
- ☞ Press **Ctrl-T** and choose a larger or smaller format. It is also possible to enlarge or reduce the text object, or to stretch it.

The circle and the text are now linked to each other by means of a so-called **dynamic link**. This is not the same as combining or grouping. Blending also made use of this kind of link. You will see this if you wanted to move the circle for instance. The text would be moved along with it. You can break this link by selecting **Separate** from the **Arrange** menu.

☞ Now select the text and then **Separate** from the **Arrange** menu.
☞ Click on the inner circle.
☞ Click on the **Outline tool** and choose the line thickness second from the left. The line is made thicker. The status bar shows: **Outline: 0.028 inches**.
☞ Do the same to the outer circle.

We shall now fill in the inner circle.

☞ Select the inner circle and then the **Filling tool**. Choose a grey tint. The inner circle is filled in. The word 'THE' has disappeared under this filling. The filling has to be placed in the background. Press **Shift-PgDn**.

The following modern eye-catching logo is the result:

Artistic text and paragraph text

This type of text which we have used for the logo is referred to as **artistic text** by CorelDRAW. CorelDRAW seems to have a good insight into what we are up to! The disadvantage of using artistic text is that you cannot use more than 250 characters (including commas, dots, spaces etc.) In addition, you must type the text in CorelDRAW itself.

But you can also enter text in CorelDRAW in another way. This is so-called **paragraph text**. This has the advantage that you can use up to 4000 characters and you can also **import** text from WordPerfect or Write or Word for instance. In addition, you can easily create broad or narrow columns when using paragraph text. This is because when you apply stretching and squeezing, it is not the letters which are altered, but the size of the block which you have made. In that case, the number of words placed on one line is altered to suit the width of the line.

We shall examine how paragraph text works.

- ☞ Begin on a new page.
- ☞ Click on the **Text tool**.
- ☞ Click anywhere on the page, hold down the left mouse button and draw a frame. Release the mouse button.

Artistic text and paragraph text 151

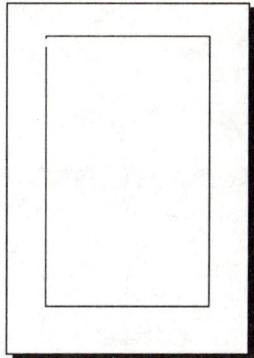

You now see the text frame on the page. The Status bar shows: **Text on Layer 1**. You can type text in this frame, and you can also import it. We shall now import text. We presume that you have created a text in a word processing program and that you have saved this text as **DOS text** or **ASCII text** under the name BUSKER.TXT. Thus, it must be text without formatting codes, in other words, without codes determining the text layout.

Note: You can of course, just type this text now. The full text is shown on page 155. We are using this text as an example, but you can also choose any other text of your own if you like.

- Select **Import** from the **File** menu.
- Select **Text, *.TXT** from the List Files of Type section. (Click on the arrow pointing downwards and then on the relevant choice.)
- Go to the Directories section and specify the directory where your text is stored.
- The Text files from this directory will be shown

in the Files section. Click on the required file and then on **OK**.

The result looks something like this:

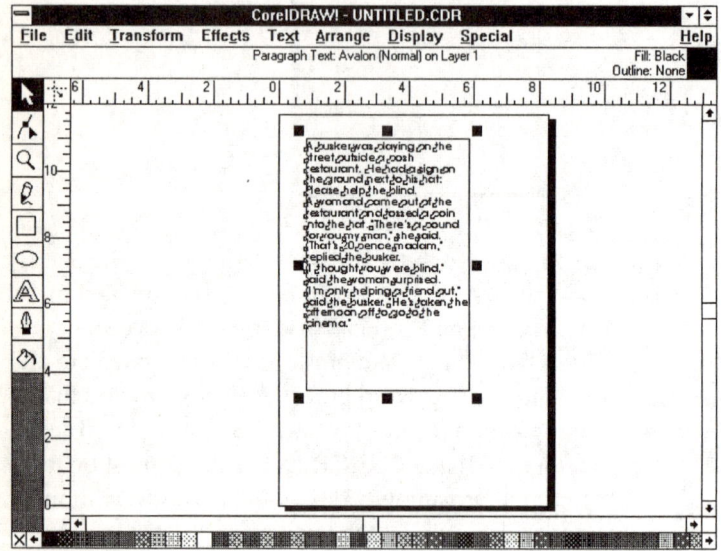

The text frame is regarded by CorelDRAW as being a normal object. Accordingly, you can rotate, enlarge, reduce, mirror it etc. If you press **Ctrl-T** you can edit the text, just as you can with artistic text.

☞ Make the frame narrower. You will see that the letters do not become smaller; there are fewer words per line.
☞ Press **Ctrl-T**. This window appears:

Artistic text and paragraph text 153

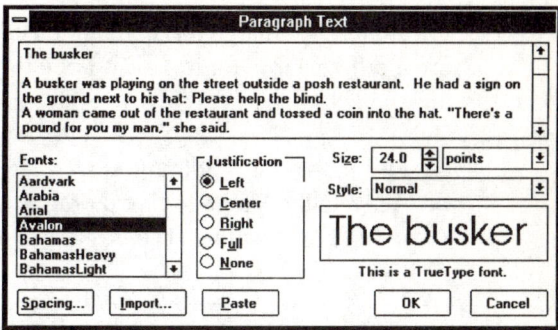

This window resembles the artistic text window. One important difference is that you can also import text using this window (instead of using **Import** from the **File** menu).

☞ Select the **France** font, **Size: 14 points**. In the **Justification** section, click on **Full** and click on **OK**.

If you now zoom out a little, your screen will look like this:

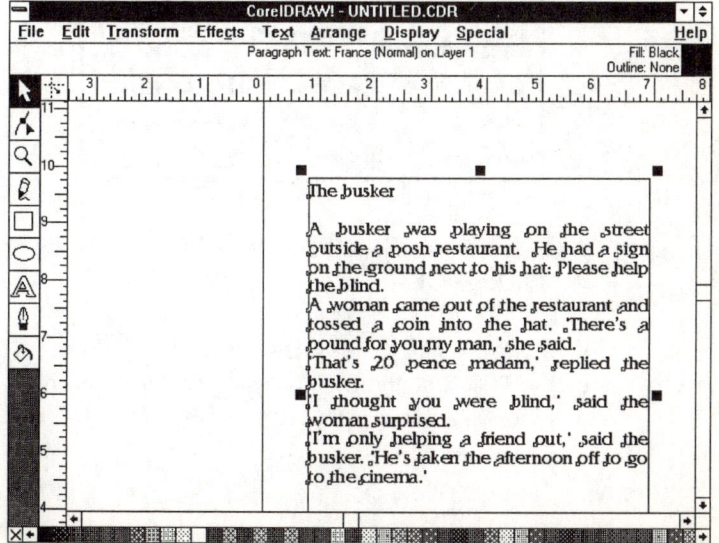

We shall now enlarge the size of the heading and use a different font for it. This is done by means of the Shape tool.

☞ Ensure that the text frame is selected.
☞ Activate the **Shape tool** and drag a frame around the heading (The busker).

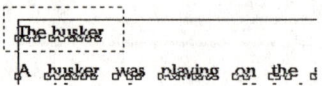

The white blocks under the letters (similar to nodes) now become black.

☞ Double click on one of the black blocks. This window appears:

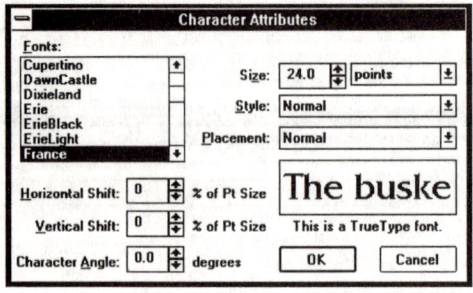

☞ Select **SwitzerlandBlack**, Size **20 points**.
☞ Click on **OK**.

If you now make the blocks invisible by clicking on the **Pick tool** and then pressing **Esc**, the screen will look like this when you zoom in a little:

Artistic text and paragraph text 155

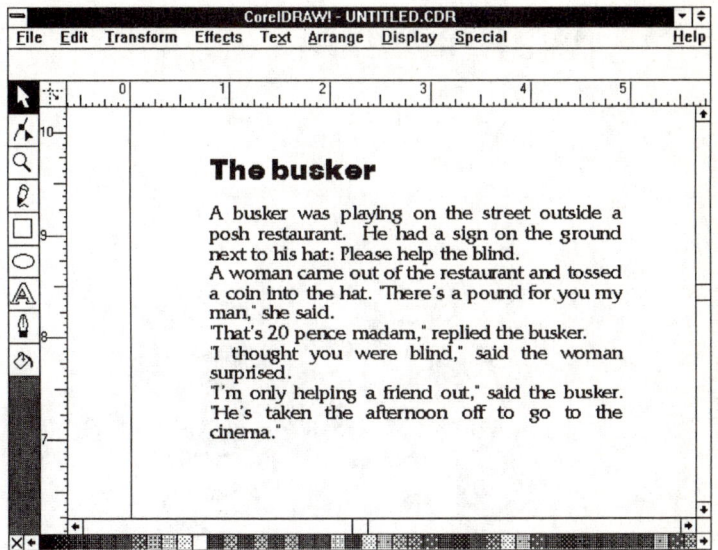

The **Character Attributes** box enables you to move or slant individual letters or words quite easily. That can also be done using the cursor.

The **Text** roll-up menu also works with paragraph text. Try it out. It will do no harm and you do not need to save the results if you are not satisfied.

If you look closely at the text, you will see that some spaces are a little larger than others. Those on the first line are wider than those on the fourth. This is due to the full justification which stretches the spaces so that the lines are filled with text to the right-hand margin (unless you have pressed Enter of course). If you do not want this effect, select the text and press **Ctrl-T**. Change the justification to **Left**. Try out all the options. It is very interesting and, as mentioned, it can do no harm.

7 Wallpapering

We shall now discuss **filling**.

If you click on the **Filling tool**, a pop-out menu appears as you already know. We have already dealt with fountain filling and with the grey tints which you can produce.

The Fill roll-up menu

If you open the Filling tool menu, you can click on the second box from the left. A roll-up menu then appears which enables you to apply filling easily and quickly.

Two-colour patterns

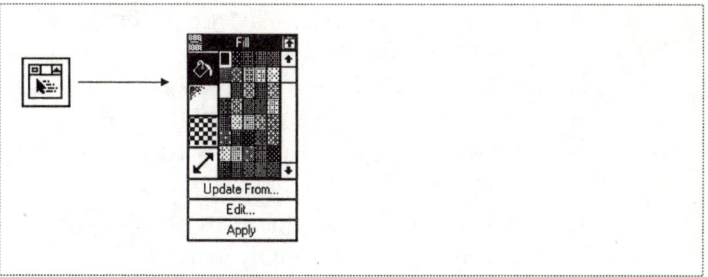

We shall now deal with the following two boxes from the pop-out menu:

The left one is for two-colour patterns and the right one is for filling patterns.

Two-colour patterns

☞ Begin on a new page and draw a circle (using Ellipse tool, holding down Ctrl).
☞ Click on the **Fill tool** and then on the **two-colour pattern** box, which looks like a chess board). This window appears:

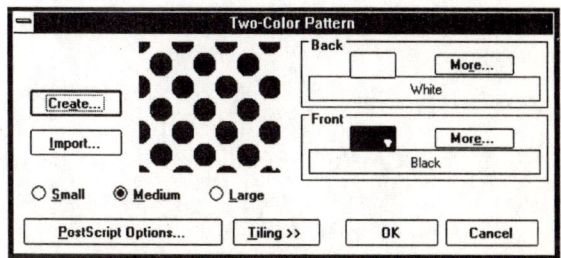

Here you can choose a pattern by clicking in the box with the spots and then choosing one of the options provided. Click on the arrows pointing downwards to see more options. This box works just like the Symbols box we saw earlier.

☞ Click on the box with the spots and move through the symbols until you reach the second last one. Double click on it to choose it (or click once on it and then on **OK**.
☞ Now click on **OK** in the **Two-Color Pattern** box.

The filling will look like this:

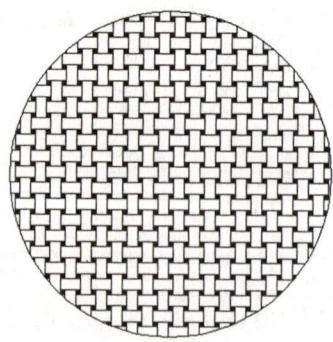

A very interesting feature is that you can not only make use of existing patterns, you can also create patterns yourself and you can **import** a pattern.

☞ Select the circle, click on the **Fill tool** and then on the **two-colour pattern** box. Then click on **Create**. You will immediately see what is possible. By clicking on the pattern you can apply new black areas; the boxes at the right

Two-colour patterns

determine the area being altered. Try this out yourself later. You can always click on **Cancel** if you are not satisfied.

☞ Now click on **Cancel**.

☞ Click on **Import**. The following window appears:

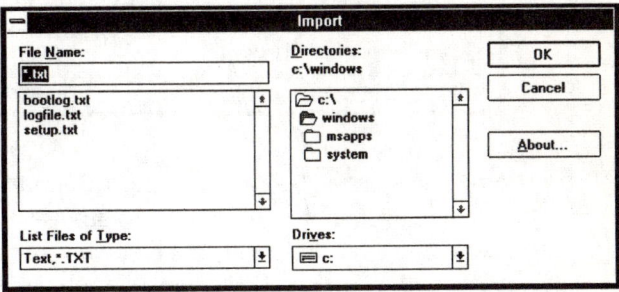

You can now **import** a drawing you have made to use it as filling. This works in the same way as importing, only it is now imported as a **filling pattern**.

We want to import our self-portrait which we made earlier. But we do not want to have the filling which we then applied, otherwise it will become one grey blob.

If your **Import** dialog box still shows Text in the List Files of Type section, change this to CorelDRAW, *.CDR. Change the Directories section to **c:\coreldrw\draw** where your self-portrait is stored. Now choose the first version of your portrait, the one without filling.

☞ Click on **selfport.cdr** in the list.

The self-portrait appears as a pattern in the **Two-Color Pattern** window:

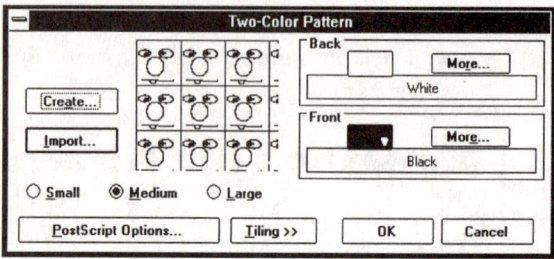

Now click on the button for **Large**. This portrait is now included in the collection of patterns which you can see by clicking on the box with spots. Do this shortly. First we shall complete our pattern.

☞ Click on **OK**. The circle is now filled with this pattern.

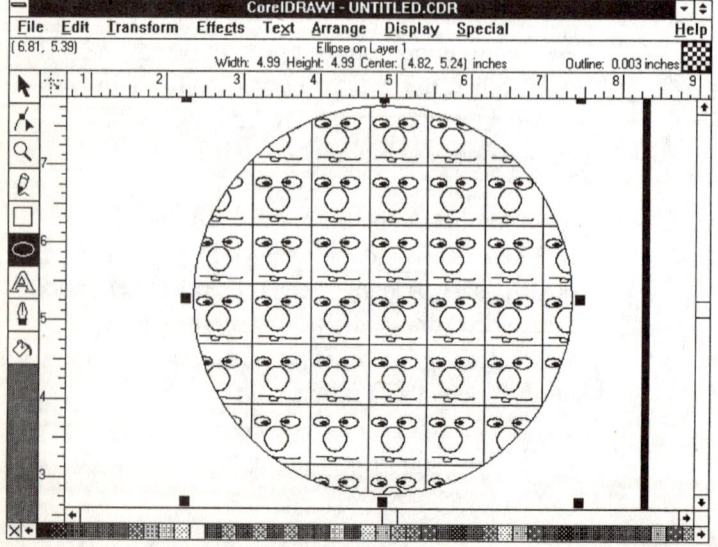

Great eh? But have you noticed that CorelDRAW has made the head square? This is because a fill pattern is always square.

 ### Adjusting the size of the tiles

*If you select the **Tiling** option from the **Two-Color Pattern** dialog window, you can determine exactly how large the 'tiles' should be. In this way you can see that the segments are not square. Experiment with this.*

You can fill all kinds of objects with patterns, even letters:

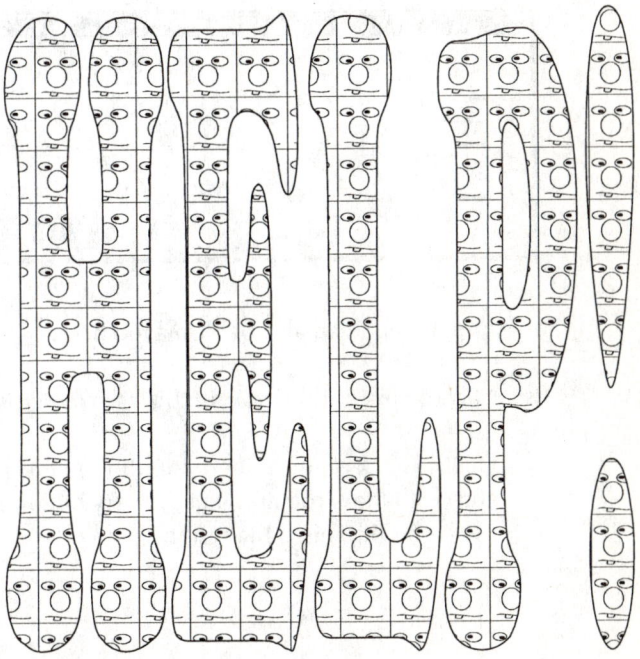

Full-colour patterns

Full-colour patterns are very similar to two-colour patterns. An important difference is that fill patterns can have **more colours**.

☞ Begin on a new page and draw a large square. Zoom in.
☞ Click on the **Fill tool** and then on this box:

This window then appears:

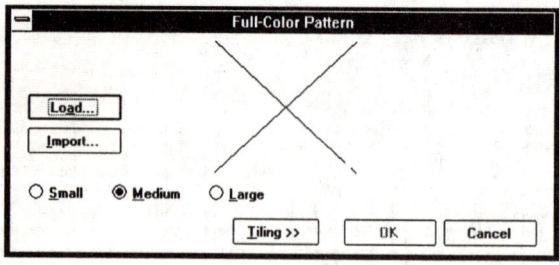

A pop-out menu can also be displayed here.

☞ Click on the sample box, in this case the cross itself.
☞ Double click on the pattern fourth from the end (with the scroll arrow at the very bottom).
☞ Click on **OK**. This is the result:

Creating a pattern yourself 163

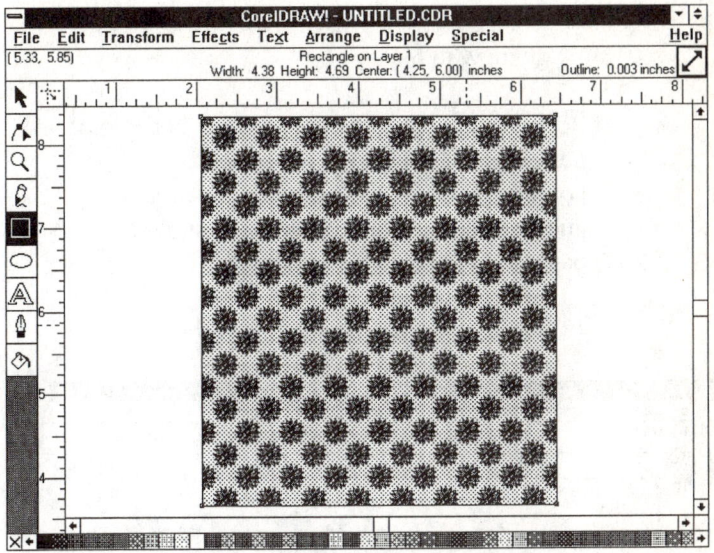

You can also import drawings with these full-colour patterns. In addition, you can also load a pattern by entering its **name** when you have chosen the **Load** option in the **Full-Color Pattern** dialog window.

Creating a pattern yourself

You can also create a pattern yourself. We shall outline how this is done.

- ☞ Begin on a new page.
- ☞ Activate the **Symbol tool** and place the following symbols next to one another: Household **32**, Animals **14**, Transportation **118**, Tools **1**, Festive **6**, Space **14**, Food **6**, Business & Government **10** and Music **4**.

☞ Select all objects except the scissors and fill them with black.

You will see that some objects only become partially black. This is because some objects consist of combined curves, as you probably already guessed. (If you want to refresh your memory, read pages 126-127 again.)

☞ Order the symbols roughly as shown:

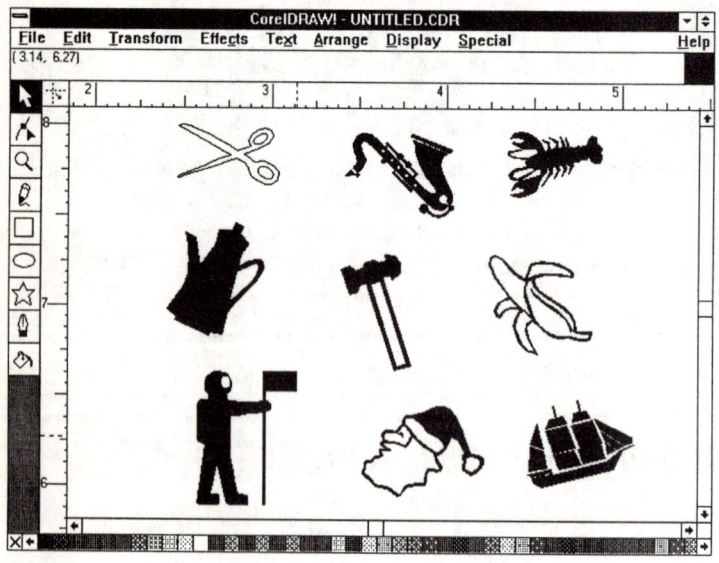

☞ Open the **Special** menu and choose the **Create Pattern** option. The following window appears:

Creating a pattern yourself 165

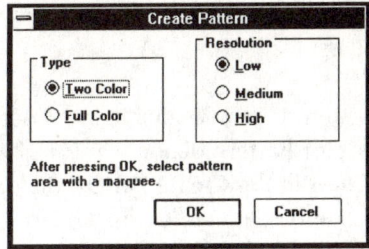

☞ Select **High** in the Resolution section and click on **OK**.

The cursor now changes into a large cross. This enables you to indicate which area is to be used as a pattern. Select the area shown by dragging a frame round your symbols. Place the intersection of the lines at the top left corner above the symbols and drag the mouse downwards to the right:

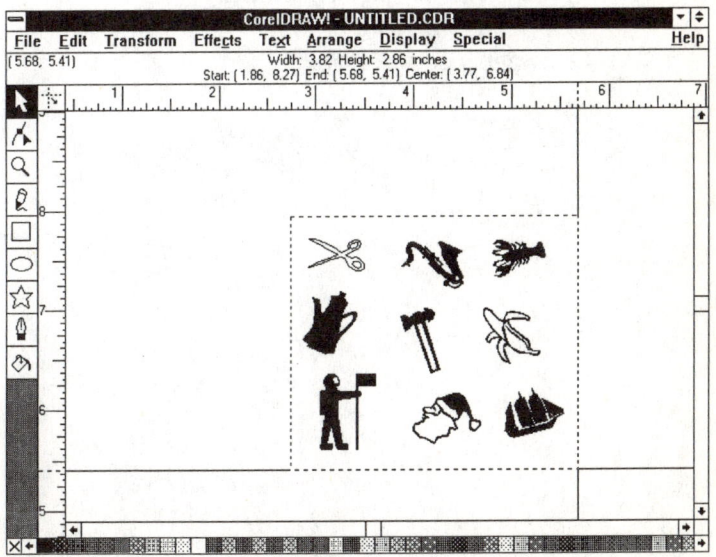

☞ Click on **OK** in the window which then appears.

The pattern is now available as an option in the **Two-Color Pattern** dialog window. If you choose **Full-Color** in the **Create Pattern** dialog box, you have to enter a name for the pattern you create. This pattern is then included as an option in the **Full-Color Pattern** dialog window.

We can now finally get down to creating our own wallpaper.

☞ Begin on a new page.
☞ Make a rectangle which is almost as large as the page and then remove the outline.
☞ Activate the **Two-Color Pattern** menu and select the pattern we have just created.
☞ Select **Large** and click on **OK**.

Our wallpaper is available!

Creating a pattern yourself

Rounding off

Yes, we have completed our explanation. Of course, CorelDRAW is a program which is so rich in features and facilities that we cannot hope to explain everything within the scope of this book. But if you have followed the explanations and the exercises consistently, you will already be able to create remarkably attractive drawings. And keep in mind, the more you try, the more you will learn.

Have a lot of fun!

And, oh yes, we didn't want to mention it earlier (we didn't want to get in your way), but there are a great deal of drawings available in CorelDRAW. These are stored in the subdirectories of the C:\CORELDRW\DRAW\CLIPART directory. If you have CorelDRAW on CD ROM, you will have even more sample drawings.

Index

A4 paper 66
active (tool) 19, 21, 24
alignment 109
Arrange menu 53, 79
arranging objects (to front/to back) 53, 96
artistic text 140, 150

bitmap 129
black, making an object ~ 44
black blocks (around an object) 24
blending objects 133
BMP files 129
breaking combined objects 79, 90, 126
Bézier 112-114, 117

CDR file extension 18, 40
circle 19, 22
closed path 55
co-ordinates 68
colour palette 19, 29
colour screen 12
colour, removing ~ 54
colouring in an object 52
colours (outline) 44
combined objects 79
combining objects 83, 126
control points 114
copying an object 30, 84
Corel Graphics window 16
CorelCHART 13
CorelSHOW 13
CorelTRACE 13
Ctrl key 22, 36, 83
cursor 20
curve 32, 73, 79, 83, 92, 114-125

curve versus line 117

deselecting an object 35
Display menu 69
double click 16
duplicating an object 30, 84, 85, 86
dynamic link 148

Effects menu 143
Ellipse tool 19, 20
enlarging an object 28
enlarging the CorelDRAW window 17
exiting CorelDRAW 39

F1 (help) 101
F2 (zooming in) 76
F3 (zooming out) 76
F4 (bringing everything into view) 87
F9 (preview) 59
File menu 39, 42
Fill tool 19, 55
filling 156
fit text to path 146
fixing the page 132
font 139
font, changing the ~ 141, 153, 154
fountain fill 56
full-colour pattern 56, 162

graphic program 9
grey tints 44, 56
grid origin point 69
gridlines 102
grouping objects 126
guidelines 105

Help menu 101

importing (as a filling pattern) 159

importing a drawing 127
importing text 150, 153

layer 48, 52
Letter (paper size) 67
letters 137
line 124
line (straight) 122
line thickness 44
line versus curve 117
linear fill 57

magnetic guidelines 107
magnifying glass 74
marquee rectangle 46
menu bar 18
mirror image 81
mistakes (correcting them) 22, 26
moving 23
MS-DOS 10

new drawing 66
no fill 56
node 32, 78, 92, 114-125
Node Edit menu 92, 116, 118, 120-122

objects, all ~ on the screen 87
opening a drawing 42
outline 137
outline pen settings 44
Outline tool 19, 44

page 20
page settings 66
paragraph text 150
patterns 157
patterns, creating ~ 163
Pencil tool 19, 31, 113, 122
perspective 143

PgUp/PgDn	96
Pick tool	19, 24, 30
pop-up menu	44
PostScript	56
printing	36
quitting CorelDRAW	39
radial fill	57
Rectangle tool	19, 33
reducing the size of an object	28
remove outline	44
removing colour	54
roll-up menu	44, 56
roll-up menu (Blend)	133
roll-up menu (Fill)	156
roll-up menu (Fit Text To Path)	146
roll-up menu (Text)	142, 155
rotating an object	60, 80, 97
rulers	68, 70
saving	39, 64
screen	12
scroll bar	19
selected (object)	23
selecting (an object)	27, 51, 74
selecting several things	46
selection, undoing a ~	35
settings of CorelDRAW	11, 66
Shape tool	19, 48, 92, 115, 123-125
Shift key	47, 110, 125
skew	111
snap to grid	105
snap to guidelines	107
squeezing an object	34
standard settings	11
starting CorelDRAW	14
starting Windows	15
status bar	18

stretching an object 34, 82
Symbol tool 71
symbols 71, 89

Tab key 51
text 137
Text tool 19, 71, 138
text, changing ~ 141
thickness of a line 44
tick (in front of menu options) 69
tiles, adjusting the size of ~ 161
TIP symbol 12
title bar 18, 43
toolbox 18
Transform menu 81
two-colour pattern 56, 157

undoing a selection 35
undoing rotation, skewing & mirroring 112
ungrouping objects 127
uniform fill 56

VGA screen 12

white, making an object ~ 44
Windows 10, 15, 66
wireframe 59

Zoom tool 19, 74
zooming in 75
zooming in (using the mouse) 78
zooming out 76

also in this series:

Programming with QBasic
be an expert!

If you want the computer to carry out your own special wishes, you have to program it. This means that you create a list of commands which the computer has to perform. Of course, you must do this according to particular rules, in a certain language. The language we deal with in this book is called QBasic. When you get your computer, you are also supplied with QBasic. Programming in this language can be done quickly and easily. The results of your work are immediately obvious.
When you have finished this book, you will not only be able to write your own programs, you will have also created the following programs:

- a program to make your computer beep
- a program to capture hearts
- a program to play the game of Mastermind
- a program to arrange the sports results
- a program to keep track of your pocket money and to write menus
- a program for making tunes.

There is something for everybody. There's a whole world just waiting to be programmed!

ISBN 1-85365-346-2

also in this series:

Word Processing with WordPerfect
be an expert!

Everybody wants to work with WordPerfect. But... how do you go about it? If you use this book, you can find out how WordPerfect enables you to apply all kinds of word processing features. For instance you can write your text in columns just as in newspapers or magazines, you can move whole passages of text, you can even place drawings in your letters and documents.

It does not matter if you have not used this program before - everything will be explained right from the very beginning.
And when you have finished this book, you will be ready to step into the world of Fleet Street!

Some of the exercises in this book:

- making an invitation to a party
- changing the appearance of the letters (bold, italics, underlined, size, spacing etc.)
- using the automatic spelling check
- writing punishment lines automatically
- how to print the text.

ISBN 1-85365-351-9

also in this series:

Word Processing with Word for Windows
be an expert!

If you have Windows on your computer, there is no better word processing program than Word for Windows. It is clear and easy to operate. But how do you learn the basic skills? If you use this book, you can find out how to apply many word processing features: you can create text in columns just as in newspapers and magazines, use various types of letters and signs, even place drawings in your documents and letters, and much more.

It does not matter if you have not worked with this program before - everything is explained in detail right from the very beginning. When you have worked through this book, the quality of your letters and documents will surprise your friends, parents and teachers!

Some of the exercises in this book:

- making an invitation to a party
- changing the appearance of letters (large, small, bold, underlined, italics, spacing etc.)
- how to print the text
- using the automatic spelling check
- writing a 'real' letter.

ISBN 1-85365-341-1